ROGERS MEMORIAL LIBRARY

A Book Sale How-To Guide

For Reference

Not to be taken from this room

D1293842

ALA Editions purchases fund advocacy, awareness, and
accreditation programs for library professionals worldwide.

For Reference

Not to be taken from this room

A Book Sale How-To Guide

More Money, Less Stress

Pat Ditzler • JoAnn Dumas

American Library Association

Chicago   2012

© 2012 by the American Library Association. Any claim of copyright is subject to applicable limitations and exceptions, such as rights of fair use and library copying pursuant to Sections 107 and 108 of the U.S. Copyright Act. No copyright is claimed for content in the public domain, such as works of the U.S. government.

Printed in the United States of America
16 15 14 13 12   5 4 3 2 1

Extensive effort has gone into ensuring the reliability of the information in this book; however, the publisher makes no warranty, express or implied, with respect to the material contained herein.

ISBNs: 978-0-8389-1074-0 (paper); 978-0-8389-9403-0 (PDF). For more information on digital formats, visit the ALA Store at alastore.ala.org and select eEditions.

Library of Congress Cataloging-in-Publication Data available at http://catalog.loc.gov

Book design in Berlin Sans FB and Oranda BT by Kirstin Krutsch.

⊗ This paper meets the requirements of ANSI/NISO Z39.48-1992 (Permanence of Paper).

To the Lancaster (PA) Public Library, the Potsdam (NY) Public Library, and the Oro Valley (AZ) Public Library. These libraries are the beneficiaries of our book sales, as well as the proving grounds for the advice and materials included here.

ROGERS MEMORIAL LIBRARY

ROGERS MEMORIAL LIBRARY

Contents

WEB See alaeditions.org/webextras for blank, reproducible versions of the sample documents shown in this book.

Acknowledgments

We wish to thank our families and friends for living the book sales with us. Those who know us cannot avoid being involved in our glorious book sale adventures.

Our hats off to all the volunteers around the country who devote time and energy to making public libraries a vital and growing part of their communities.

Introduction

Even as libraries successfully evolve in our technology-based world and continue to serve an ever-increasing number of people, the funding for these vital institutions is being assaulted. State funding cuts and federal program cutbacks have resulted in budget deficits, forcing libraries to cut book budgets, curtail hours of operation, and lay off staff—a woeful situation.

Yet, individually, people are passionate about their local library and believe in its mission. You'll find that, if asked, members of your own community will be happy to donate books from their personal collections and can be a huge source of free books. *A Book Sale How-To Guide* is designed to help you take advantage of your patrons' willingness to provide in-kind support. It offers a tested and successful formula for making money for local libraries in a practical and fun way—a library book sale.

THE BENEFITS OF A BOOK SALE

Book sales can help alleviate funding deficits while fostering a healthy library volunteer community. By holding a successful library book sale, you can make a difference in your own community by

- offering affordable books to everyone, but particularly local citizens;
- raising enormous amounts of money for the library in a fun, satisfying way;
- promoting a rare sense of community that is unbelievable in scope;

- developing lifelong friendships—an amazing camaraderie grows around sale activities;
- developing skills of volunteers that can translate into lucrative jobs or a more fulfilling lifestyle for them;
- providing enormous savings for the library because of the opportunity to put some of the donated books directly into the permanent collection;
- becoming the largest recycling effort in your community;
- generating commercial traffic at local restaurants, hotels, stores, tourist attractions, and the like from book sale customers;
- creating a positive reflection on your community as a caring place to live and work.

And while our assumption in preparing this guide is that proceeds will benefit your local library, the material included can also be adapted for other nonprofit or for-profit organizations.

THE BENEFITS OF FOLLOWING THIS GUIDE

This book was born out of a need to share the knowledge gained over many years at the Lancaster (PA) Public Library book sale, now in its fifty-seventh year. In 2010 the Lancaster book sales raised $170,000, bringing their cumulative total book sale profits to over $2.5 million.

The Lancaster Library Friends used their extensive book sale knowledge to help the Potsdam (NY) Friends of the Library group start a small book sale modeled after Lancaster's huge sale. Success with the sale in Potsdam proved the value of sharing this information with others. With Lancaster's help, the first year's proceeds in Potsdam ($6,100) far exceeded their expectations. It took Lancaster seventeen years to make over $6,000 from one sale!

Potsdam's first foray into ongoing book sales began in a small way through telephone conversations with Pat Ditzler in Lancaster. She encouraged her sister, JoAnn Dumas, to approach the Potsdam Friends group with the idea of holding a book sale. This would mean finding a sorting site and also soliciting book donations from the public. Luckily, the Friends' president was very excited and willing to work toward that end.

Using Lancaster's documented book sale information, Potsdam held their first sale in a church basement, with all the Friends (six people!) working very hard. The Potsdam Library director was thrilled with their fundraising success.

When JoAnn moved to Arizona in 2002, the brand new Oro Valley Public Library was just about to open. She immediately joined the Friends group, which had already held two small book sales under a tent in conjunction with a local arts council. The book sale committee reorganized, and they too began using Lancaster's book sale model. Using Lancaster's techniques, they recruited new volunteers, increased book donations, learned how to research and price books, and held their first major book sale in October 2002. Oro Valley Friends now have two large, very organized, professional, and well-attended sales each year, and have also expanded their horizons into other selling opportunities. These efforts raised over $80,000 in 2010.

Throughout this guide, you will find specific "Details from Our Sales" for each of these libraries, which show how the information provided has worked in practice and, often, how it has been modified to meet the needs of the individual sales.

SALES HISTORIES FOR BOOK SALES REFERENCED IN THIS GUIDE

Lancaster (PA) Public Library

1954 (first year) sale	$153
2008 sale	$180,000
2008 books sold	250,000
Total income of all sales to date	$2,250,000

Potsdam (NY) Public Library

1999 (first year) sale	$6,100

Oro Valley (AZ) Public Library

2002 (first year) sale	$10,000
2008 sale	$66,000
2009 sale	$80,352

ORGANIZATIONS THAT TYPICALLY SPONSOR BOOK SALES

Friends of the Library

Organizations in support of libraries have a long history. The Library Company of Philadelphia was started by Benjamin Franklin in 1731 to "render the benefit of reading more common" and is still in operation today. The first Friends of the Library was started in Paris in 1913, and the first American branch was organized in Berkeley, California, in 1930. Friends of Libraries U.S.A. is now part of the Association of Library Trustees, Advocates, Friends and Foundations, which is in turn a division of the American Library Association.

Local library Friends organizations vary in structure, purpose, and activities based on their own communities and local needs. These organizations help their libraries by raising funds for special books, periodicals, and other unbudgeted items and amenities that help keep the library current and make it a welcoming place in the community. The Friends provide volunteer help to the library in many ways, including assistance with programs and public relations, both of which keep the library prominent in the community. Friends groups are advocates of the library. While few would argue against the necessity of the library, Friends are proactive in arguing for it, committed to making the community aware of the library and its importance to the

vitality of the community. Particularly in these times of underfunding, the dollars the Friends raise have become an important part of the library's financial picture.

AAUW

The American Association of University Women (AAUW) sponsors many book sales around the country and, in fact, started the Lancaster book sale. When the group decided to focus its resources on national AAUW issues, the Friends took over the Lancaster book sale. The transition was an easy one, as the same people who worked on the book sale under AAUW continued their volunteer efforts by joining the Friends. The difference is that now the library is guaranteed 100 percent of the book sale proceeds.

Women's Clubs, University Organizations, and Other Clubs

Many successful book sales are run by a myriad of non-profit organizations. The sponsoring group is immaterial, as long as everyone agrees on who gets the profits. While getting reasonably priced books into the hands of the public is laudable any way you can accomplish it, there are undeniably added benefits for the book-reading public when the proceeds go to your public library.

However you decide to organize your group, take special care to ensure that those who know and run the book sale have ample authority to make simple decisions concerning the sale. Don't jeopardize the success of your sale by getting bogged down with dozens of approval levels and having to get total consensus from a governing board or huge group of Friends. Keep it simple!

ABOUT THIS BOOK

A Book Sale How-To Guide covers every aspect of book sales, from book storage to sorting and pricing books, volunteer recruitment, sale-day issues, money matters . . . and so much more. If you've never held a book sale before, everything you need to develop a book sale is here, from start to finish. If you've held book sales and want to increase your fund-raising dollars,

WHO'S IN CHARGE?

The book sales that form the basis for this guide are under the auspices of the Friends of the Library groups. The Lancaster sale is run by a special book sale committee, which reports to the larger Friends group. Because the Potsdam Friends is a very small organization (but growing steadily!) the entire group handles the book sale as well as all other Friends activities. Oro Valley has a director of book sale operations, which is a permanent Friends board of directors position.

this book can help you build a sustained money-making operation.

A book sale has various phases that in many ways mirror those involved in producing a stage play. The chapters of this book are organized to help the reader identify the various aspects of the "production."

As with the production of a show, much work happens before anyone enters the theater on opening night. The important point, though, is never to lose sight of what this venture is all about. Thus chapter 1 is titled "The Main Attraction" and details how your group can gather the many books you'll need for sales. Chapter 2, "Setting the Scene," provides guidance on where to price, sort, and store your donations. Chapter 3, "Directing the Show," gives organizing principles for book sale committees. Cultivating a volunteer base of support is the lifeblood of a good sale, thus chapter 4, "Casting Call," discusses general recruitment. Chapter 5, "Production," addresses the major (and majorly fun) undertaking of sorting books and other media. Guidance on how to set prices to get the best value for both you and your book sale patrons is covered in chapter 6, "Ticket Price." Chapter 7, "Venue and Promotion," guides you through presale activities, including how to make your publicity shine. And then chapter 8, "Showtime," covers conducting the actual book sale from setup to cleanup. Here you'll find direction on how to make all aspects of your sale day function smoothly, and how to manage sticky situations—rare but not unheard of. Handling funds is serious business and is addressed in chapter 9, "Box Office Receipts." Chapter 10 is, of course, "Encore! Encore!," which explores Internet sales and other opportunities for revenue during the year that can augment a main book sale event. The many forms and figures provided are yours to adapt to your local operation to help you develop your own unique take on this fabulous fund-raiser.

WHAT CAN YOU ACCOMPLISH?

The Friends of the Lancaster Public Library were the largest contributors to the library's 1995 capital campaign and continue to be a huge revenue resource in the library's annual budget. The Potsdam Friends are dedicating funds to a library expansion. Friends of the Oro Valley Public Library book sales have purchased computers, outdoor furniture and a patio roof, programming, new books for the library collection, and most recently a Smart Board and a public address system.

1

The Main Attraction

Getting Book Donations

 TIP

Do not keep or sell videos, cassettes, or CDs that have been recorded by a donor. It is impossible to review the content and quality of these items. They need to be discarded.

A constant supply of generous donations is the key to successful book sales. Without book donations, you have no sale! Our experience has been that people want to donate their books. You just need to give them the opportunity. Once you start receiving book donations, word of mouth spreads the news quickly through the community.

Kick off your efforts by issuing a press release that solicits books as well as donations of compact discs, videos, audiobooks, and records (fig. 1.1). These electronic items sell very well and bring new customers to your sales. Radio and TV stations and newspapers are usually happy to give time and space for library activities. Especially in smaller communities, your weekly newspaper may be willing to donate space for a standing box ad stating that the Friends group is looking for books for resale to benefit the library. Include information about when and where to donate books and a contact number for questions or for pickup requests.

Enlist help from other organizations and businesses! Print the content from your newspaper ad, perhaps with a small map, on bookmarks and ask local businesses to keep them by their registers. Place brochures and posters in waiting rooms and in shop windows, as well as in prominent community areas.

FROM: Jane Doe, Publicity Chair
SUBJECT: Lancaster Public Library Book Sale Accepting Book Donations
DATE: March 15, 2000

FOR IMMEDIATE RELEASE
Donations will be accepted for the Lancaster Public Library Book Sale on Saturday, April 3, from 10 a.m. to 1 p.m. at the Book ReSort located at 650 Janet Avenue, Lancaster. Donations are also accepted Monday and Wednesday mornings from 10 a.m. until noon.

Volunteers will be available on the first Saturday of each month to help unload donated books. There is ample free parking, easy access to the facility, and plenty of staff ready to help.

People bringing large quantities of books should bring them in cardboard boxes. All donations must be in good condition. Children's books are urgently needed. Records, videos, sheet music, cassette tapes, and CDs are also accepted. Textbooks should be no older than 10 years. Reader's Digest condensed books and magazines cannot be accepted.

Donations are accepted at the Book ReSort on the first Saturday of each month, and the Friends of the Library prefer that donations be made at the Book ReSort. However, anyone unable to drop off books at this time should bring them to the rear of the Lancaster Public Library, Monday through Friday, between the hours of 8 a.m. and 5 p.m.

For more information and directions, please call the Book ReSort at (717) 493-9327.

Figure 1.1 WEB
Sample book drive press release. Press releases should be printed on official Friends or Library letterhead.

Offer your donors a signed donation receipt (fig. 1.2) that they can use as proof of a charitable contribution. Do not give dollar estimates for these donations, but rather provide price suggestions that the donors themselves can assign. We suggest the following:

hardbacks—$2
paperbacks—50 cents
videos—$1
audiobooks and DVDs $2
LPs—50 cents to $1
newer items of any kind—add $1

Whatever values you choose, keep them low. Some items you will be able to sell for more than your estimate, some for less, and some not at all. The values provided above are very rough but, on average, very fair estimates.

Play on your community's sense of environmentalism. Lancaster's marketing strategy emphasizes that their book sale is the largest recycling effort in the county.

In fact they have resold some of the same volumes again year after year, as shown by sales receipts found in donated books. Community members are redonating the volumes they have purchased at prior book sales! This phenomenon is also happening in the Potsdam and Oro Valley libraries.

Appeal to your donors' love of the library. Those with a passion for the library will come through with some unbelievable book donations. Opening a recent box of Lancaster donations, volunteers pulled out amazing books—colonial architecture of the East Coast, *The Socinian Creed* by John Edwards (circa 1697), and an autographed book by Richard Nixon. Lancaster made a lot of money on this one donation, which the donor could have sold to a used bookstore, but instead chose to donate to his local library. Oro Valley recently received the complete personal library of a Friend who was moving out of state. The eighty boxes of beautiful books he donated have already brought in hundreds of dollars to the library's benefit.

SNOWBIRD DONORS

If you are in a mild and sunny climate, don't overlook soliciting donations from the snowbirds—people who have a permanent home elsewhere but spend the winter months in your area. Many will be happy to donate their recently purchased books to the Friends rather than store them in their small winter homes or ship them back to their permanent residences. These current, like-new books are a welcome addition for any book sale.

Identify community members who may be downsizing or moving to retirement homes and, sadly, will have no room for their lifetime collection of beloved books. They will be happy to know that their cherished books will benefit the library and the community. Similarly, identify those who must forgo creating personal collections, such as college students or seasonal residents.

Go where the goods are. Visit garage sales and ask that any "good books" left over after the garage sale be donated to the library. If you can offer to have someone pick up the books, you increase your chances of getting them. Before you ask for the leftover books, be sure that the books you ask for are salable. Some garage sale items may not be of acceptable quality. See the example garage sale donation request (fig. 1.3), which is designed to allow you to tear off a slip to give to the garage sale person with your contact information.

SCHOOL BOOK DRIVES

As sales increase, you will likely find that there are never enough children's and teen books to meet customer expectations. One way to address this is to get to know and work closely with the school librarians. Schools are often looking for good community projects and are willing partners in endeavors where students can learn about community service. A school book drive can serve this purpose and also help meet demand for good used children's and teen books at your sale.

To Whom It May Concern:

The Lancaster Public Library acknowledges receipt of _____ books donated to the library by _____

_____

_____.

If the books cannot be used in the collection, they will be turned over to the Friends of the Library for use in upcoming book sales to benefit the Lancaster Public Library.

Received by

_____

Lancaster Public Library representative

_____

Date

Figure 1.2 🕸️

Sample donation receipt. Donation receipts should be printed on official Friends or Library letterhead.

Please consider donating your leftover books to the Friends of the Potsdam Public Library book sales. All our proceeds benefit the Potsdam Public Library. Please call the number below, and we will gladly pick up the books at the end of your sale.

Call (315) 264-9999 for book donation and pickup

Figure 1.3 🕸️

Sample garage sale donation request.

School book drives are projects that individual schools run, with some basic information and tools provided to the school by the book sale committee. The schools send letters home to the parents, line up a few PTA/PTO volunteers to help with the drive, and offer incentives to the students (often resulting in some very lively competitions between classrooms).

Encouraging Schools to Participate

Send a letter to each school librarian in your library service area asking the school to sponsor a book donation drive (fig. 1.4). Encourage the school librarian to pull some books from the donations to keep for the school library before sending the rest of the books to your sale. We also suggest that for every five to ten books a student donates, the librarian allow the student to choose a book from all books collected. This way, the schools get good books for their library; the students have a personal incentive to collect donations, and they get different books to take home and read; and the book sale gets an excellent assortment of juvenile books to offer to the community at the next sale.

Dear Librarian,

The Friends of the Lancaster Public Library will again be sponsoring the annual spring book sale for the benefit of Lancaster Public Library. This year the sale will be held at the Overlook Roller Rink May 3–5, 1999.

The public donates books year-round for this sale. These books are then sold to provide inexpensive reading materials for the community, as well as to help the financial needs of the public library system. Last year our various book sales raised over $120,000 for the library!

The Friends of the Library would again like to expand the idea of public service by offering schools the opportunity to sponsor book donation drives. You, as the librarian, could select from the books collected at your school to enhance your own library collection. In addition, your students could, after making a donation of five to ten books, choose a book from those collected. Since our greatest need is always children's books, please encourage your students to donate these.

Many schools that have been involved in the past have used PTO or other volunteers to help with the book drive. Books should be collected to arrive in our warehouse by April 1 so we can sort them and take them to our May sale.

Your interest and help in this project will be greatly appreciated! A kit of materials will be sent to help you with publicity and the mechanics of carrying out your book drive. We can arrange with our library staff to pick up your packed cartons at the conclusion of the campaign. We can also provide you with boxes for the drive.

Thank you for taking the time to help provide quality reading materials for the children of Lancaster Public Library. If you would be willing to see that your school is involved in this great recycling of books, kindly return the enclosed card by Dec. 1, 2000.

I look forward to your reply.

Sincerely,

Barbara Jones
Friends of the Library
School Book Drive Coordinator

Figure 1.4 WEB
Sample school book drive letter to school librarian. Letters regarding your sale should be printed on official Friends or Library letterhead.

School Book Drive Procedure

Along with the letter to each school librarian, enclose a postcard for schools to return (fig. 1.5). Note on the postcard that if the school agrees to hold a book drive, additional information will be sent. Ask that the postage-paid cards be returned whether or not the school is going to participate.

When the book sale committee receives the postcards, send an information packet to the schools who have agreed to hold a book drive. The packet should include a letter to each librarian or book sale coordinator at the participating school (fig. 1.6); posters and bookmarks to be used during the campaign; and a sample letter for the school librarian to send home with students explaining the book drive (fig. 1.7). Set a specific time frame (about a three-month window) for when the book drive should be held. Set the end of that window no later than one month before your sale to allow time for incorporating these books into your sale.

Once the books have been collected at the school, the school librarian or book drive coordinator should call you to arrange to have the books picked up from the school and taken to your sorting facility. Ask the schools to fill out a brief report on the book drive (like the one in fig. 1.8), including the number of books collected.

Keep a list of participating schools from year to year so you can target different schools for participation in rotation. Don't forget to acknowledge participating schools as book sale supporters wherever community supporters are listed!

Details from Our Sales

Lancaster

Approximately 98 percent of Lancaster's sale books come from community donations. The other 2 percent are withdrawn volumes from the library's permanent collection. This mix of mostly donated books is a big draw to book shoppers and collectors, who are often not enchanted with ex-library copies. Some book sales have a much larger percentage of withdrawn volumes. While attending the Denver annual book sale many years ago, Pat noted a huge amount of withdrawn books in the sale. A sale committee member said that 80 percent of their sale books were withdrawn from the library's shelves. We hope that Denver has begun soliciting more donations from its huge community. In the much smaller city of Lancaster, the five trucks packed with books for the spring sale weighed in at 100,000 pounds—fifty tons!—almost all of them donated by the public.

Lancaster advertises and truly believes in our mission to get affordable books into the hands of our local citizens. Many times we have received books from estates that were settled. We also make it convenient for the public to donate books. While the library accepts book donations from the public during regular library hours, the book sale committee has set up book donation drop-off days. Donations are accepted on the first Saturday of every month and also at three other specified times during the week when we are sorting books. The donations are accepted at our sorting warehouse, with plenty of free parking and volunteers with

---

School name _____

Our school **is / is not** interested in having a book drive this year.

Contact person for book drive _____

Dates of your book drive _____

Number of posters needed _____

Number of bookmarks needed _____

Expected date for book pickup _____

Figure 1.5 [WEB]
Information to include on a school book drive response card. Enclose with request letter to schools; use a stamped postcard with your return address on the reverse.

Dear Book Drive Coordinator,

Thank you so much for helping your school collect used books for the annual Friends of the Library book sale.

Enclosed you will find the bookmarks and poster you requested. We are looking especially for children's and teen books. Your task is to coordinate the drive in your school by working with school personnel to set up the collection drive in your building. Below is a list of suggestions on items to help make a successful book drive. A committed librarian, lots of publicity, and an incentive for the students are the keys to success.

Some suggestions:
- Meet with the librarian to plan any specific activities and publicity.
- Contact the PTO to see if they will provide a lunch treat to the winning homeroom at each level.
- Prior to the book drive, send notices home to parents along with report cards.
- Locate a room parent to collect books in homerooms on each collection day.
- Consider using cafeteria tables staffed by room parents on collections days.
- Ask a local business for a prize (pocket dictionary, etc.) for the student who donates the most books.
- Ask students to place donated books in a bag labeled with their name, their homeroom, and the number of books.
- Advertise the book drive on hall bulletin boards and via the public address system.

Thank you for supporting the book drive.

Sincerely,

Figure 1.6 `WEB`

Sample school book drive letter to participating school. Letters regarding your sale should be printed on official Friends or Library letterhead.

Dear parents,

Here is a chance to weed out your bookshelves, help your school library, and help your public library.

The Friends of the Lancaster Public Library are preparing for their annual book sale, to be held in May. All proceeds of the sale benefit the Public library system. Our students are being asked to contribute good used books to this sale. Both paperbacks and hardbacks—especially children's and teen books—are welcomed. Our own school library will have first choice of the books collected to add to our school library collection.

Books will be collected between the hours of _____ and _____ on _____.

We hope you will help your children find some books for this drive. Recycling used books in good condition benefits everyone!

Sincerely,

Figure 1.7 `WEB`

Sample school book drive letter from school to parents. Include your version of this letter in the packet you send to schools. Schools should reproduce it on their own letterhead.

SCHOOL BOOK DRIVE REPORT

School _James Martin Elementary_

School book drive coordinator _Barb John_

School principal _Joyce Sands_

School librarian _Kathy Leader_

Dates of book drive _April 4, 2010 through April 11, 2010_

Total number of books collected _470_

Total number of boxes of books _8_

Number of books kept by school librarian _80_

Number of books redeemed with coupons (if applicable) _15_

Briefly discuss the details of your drive. Attach any letters, flyers, news releases, etc. that you used.

Publicity _Letters were sent home to parents in March, advising them of the book drive. The PTO also advertised in their March newsletter. Several art classes made posters to put on the bulletin boards throughout the school._

Incentives _The classroom that collected the most donated books was treated to an ice cream party. Also, for every five books that a student donated, they were allowed to select a donated book to keep. This was great fun and very popular._

Procedure _Working with our school PTO group, we received donated books from 8 to 9AM each day of the book drive. Two volunteers from the PTO helped each day. Children who brought in 5 books to donate were able to select a book of their choice from all the donations to keep. We discussed the importance of libraries in a community and also took a field trip to the Lancaster Public Library, where we got a tour of the library from the Manager of Youth Services._

On the back, please feel free to make any comments or suggestions for future book drives.

Please return this completed form, the rest of the packet, and extra bookmarks in an envelope or box with your collected books.

Figure 1.8 WEB
Sample school book drive report form.

carts to help unload donated books. Books donated at the library need to be loaded on the library truck and transported to the warehouse, so if we can entice the public to bring books directly to our warehouse, it helps out the library maintenance staff tremendously.

Potsdam

In its first year, the Potsdam Friends accepted book donations every Saturday from 10 a.m. to 1 p.m. The donations were slow in coming at first but grew quickly as word spread through the community. The first year we were getting fifteen to twenty boxes of book donations each Saturday. Many were in "gift" condition and certainly helped the quality of sale offerings. We received a large donation of 250 boxes of nice leftover books from the Lancaster Friends sale to help get our base of books up to a very healthy number. With this Lancaster donation, the first spring sale offered more than 20,000 books and attracted customers from a wide area. With the nice influx of public donations, Potsdam's books were 95 percent donated, with only 5 percent of the sale books from library withdrawals.

Oro Valley

The Oro Valley Friends receive donations daily at their two Book Shoppes. There the donations are priced and sorted (for Book Shoppe, Internet, or book sale), and those that are slated for the book sale are then taken to the sorting location to be processed. Our books are 90 percent donated and 10 percent library withdrawals. Volunteers will also pick up books in the immediate area.

The key to keeping a continuous supply of book donations coming is to make your donation site convenient, with regular hours, plenty of parking, and lots of unloading help. The public feels good about donating to the library, and you can provide the means to make this happen.

2

Setting the Scene

Site Considerations and Sorting Room Setup

For accepting, sorting, and storing books for your sale, you'll need a safe and dry, heated/air-conditioned site (depending on your region). In the beginning you may not get exactly what you want. Ideally, the same facility can be used to accept donations as well as sort and store them until your book sale. Keep in mind that books are very heavy, and you want to keep the need to move them from place to place at a minimum. Some facilities may even be adaptable to use for a small sale. There should be ample, and preferably free, parking for book donors to be able to drop off their books. Another selling point to encourage book donations is to offer help with unloading books from the donors' vehicles. Some of your donors may not be able to lift or carry books and may not bring them to you if no help is available.

Try to get a free donated space from a gracious community-minded person or business. Some ideas to consider are local empty storefronts, unused space at schools or universities, or a space in a business or industrial complex. Price is a serious consideration if you can't find a free site. Every dollar you pay for rent, heat, and utilities translates to more books you have to sell just to cover expenses. We are not opposed to begging or cajoling—whatever it takes within reason—to get donated goods and services in support of the library. Don't be shy! Many local businesses are more than willing to forgo their profits and give you services or materials at their cost.

Details from Our Sales

Lancaster

The Lancaster warehouse is called the Book ReSort, which was the winning entry of the naming contest we held. It is our third sorting facility in fifty-seven years of book sales. We started out in the basement of the library and then moved to the auditorium. Soon our space was needed for library use, and also the sale was growing. We moved to a donated basement in a local realtor's office building. Sorting and warehousing occurred at this facility, but all books were still being donated at the library and had to be trucked to our donated basement. We had to use conveyors to take the books out a small front basement window to trucks waiting to transport the books to the book sale site. Growing pains!

As the donations and sale continued to grow, a small committee was formed to find a bigger place for sorting and storage. The committee listed the criteria for a new site and found a suitable warehouse building. The Book ReSort is just six blocks away from the library and large enough to accept donations as well as sort and store the books. The ReSort also has an amazing, well-lit, year-round bookstore. Mini book sales are held at the ReSort twice a year to help pay the rental expense.

The Book ReSort is safe, secure, dry, and heated, and is a fun place to sort books. We keep a small used refrigerator there, along with a garage sale radio. There is bright fluorescent lighting, and we've hung book-related posters from the library to brighten up the sorting area. The sorted books are stored on wooden pallets awaiting transport to the spring book sale. A volunteer warehouse manager keeps the facility logistics running smoothly. Book donations are accepted at the Book ReSort during scheduled, advertised sorting/pricing sessions.

Potsdam

The first Potsdam warehouse sorting site was a donated space above an appliance store. The owner was a true gem who helped the Friends quickly find a home for their books—luckily the second-floor site had a freight elevator! The space, however, was not adequate for the long term (no heat or insulation in Northern New York), and the Friends soon settled into a facility donated by a local university. The warehouse was suitable for sorting

STORAGE ON A BUDGET

The Chandler (AZ) Friends group found a unique way to solve their storage problem. They acquired a storage pod (a self-storage container, usually on a flatbed trailer for portability) that they placed on the library's loading dock. What a great idea!

FRIENDS OF THE POTSDAM PUBLIC LIBRARY BOOK SALE WISH LIST

Handcart to move books
Filing cabinet
Coffeepot
Record player for checking quality of donated
   records
Clock
Radio
Bookshelves

Figure 2.1 [WEB]
Sample wish list.

as well as storage, with lots of room, heat, and lights, one wall of windows, and room for a tiny bookstore. Later, the university sold the building, and book sale operations moved to the basement of the Potsdam Library, where they continue their processes. The Potsdam community had become very aware of the Friends and their successful book sale activities in support of the library, and the book donations grew nicely.

Potsdam needed a few specific items for their sorting facility, so they posted a wish list (fig. 2.1). Amazingly, the sought-after items were quickly donated.

Oro Valley

In the new Oro Valley Library there was a 10,000-square-foot portion of the building as yet undeveloped. Books were sorted, priced, and stored there with no heat or air conditioning. Arizona does get rather cold in the winter, and in summer . . . well! When the library building was subsequently completed, the Friends had to find new quarters. A Friend offered a three-bedroom house with very low rental cost, which worked well for a number of years. We have now moved to a more central store-front location among other small retail shops. We have opened the front area of the building as our second bookshop, Book Shoppe Too. This facility also houses our Internet sales office and sorting operation.

The above examples show the ingenuity and creativity of Friends groups to explore opportunities and make the most of temporary or unappealing sites. Although temporary conditions may not have been ideal, these groups made the most of their situation and moved forward with longer-term goals. With any luck, you will be so successful in your book sale endeavors that in a few years you may outgrow your first facility!

The work space is where your books and your volunteers will spend a lot of time. Look carefully for a desirable site. Once you've moved and set up the site to accommodate your processes, you want to be able to stay there for a while. You will be advertising your address, and it helps if you can get established in a permanent place.

Acquiring a location that meets your needs will help your organization get a continual supply of donated books. Creating a pleasant place to work will keep your volunteers coming back to sort and price books.

SORTING ROOM SETUP AND SCHEDULING

The physical attributes of your workspace will help determine how to design your book-sorting and book-storage areas. There are some basic considerations that will help you set up an efficient operation.

Sorting Surfaces

You will need tables or other flat surfaces for sorting and pricing your books. Lancaster uses a combination of old, discarded library folding tables (they do not need to be pretty, just sturdy), a 6-foot table acquired at a cheap cost from a garage sale, and tables they commissioned a local vocational school to make for them at

 TIP

If you are lucky enough to have a telephone in the sorting facility, leave an answering machine message about upcoming sorts so volunteers are informed.

cost. Potsdam received donated tables from the library and a local business benefactor, and some tables they purchased themselves. Oro Valley also purchased 6-foot folding tables. Be creative, beg a little for the library, or use sawhorses with 4-foot sheets of plywood or an old door for a tabletop.

Alphabetical Categories

Whether you have a few or a multitude of categories, it will be easier for your sorters to find the right category box if the boxes are in alphabetical order on the sorting tables. You will likely have a few exceptions—for example, you may want to put Special Price/Rare books in a separate area for later pricing.

Informative Category Signs

The sorting categories need to be clearly marked for your sorters. Make signs and either hang them or place them securely on signposts on the tables. Lancaster uses an old clothesline and clothespins to hang signs. Oro Valley tapes category labels to the table edge and covers them with clear tape. See our sample category signs including special notes (fig. 2.2). Either laminate these signs or put them in plastic sleeves so they stay nice and bright.

Sorting Space

Leave room in the middle of the sorting area for boxes you are currently sorting. You may want to have a section near the middle of your category boxes where you put the unsorted boxes of books you will be sorting from. Sorters can then pick up a book and, after deciding on the correct category, walk to the box and deposit the book.

Sorting Supplies
Packing Boxes

Packing boxes are necessary for accumulating the books by category and storing them until your sale. You can use any type of box, including those boxes you receive donations in. However, as your sale grows and you have many books to store, having boxes of uniform size is a real plus. Stacking odd-size boxes from grocery or liquor stores can be hazardous if not done carefully, and these heavy boxes filled with books are not what you want to see tumbling down on your workers. Volunteers should not be asked to move large, heavy, or unwieldy boxes of books.

The nice sturdy boxes that gallons of spring water come in are an excellent option. Your local supermarket or drug store will be glad to give you these, as they will not have to flatten or pay to have these boxes carted away. Have a volunteer with a truck pick them up on a regular basis and deliver them to your sorting facility. Another option is to use collapsible boxes, which you can fold and store in flat stacks until needed. These flat boxes are much more compact when taking the empty boxes back to your warehouse facility after unpacking them at the book sale. Check with box suppliers for misprinted or otherwise unsellable merchandise that they may be willing to donate. Moving companies might have this type of collapsible box and may be willing to donate some gently used ones to the library.

Your best option may be file storage boxes with cutouts for your hands. These boxes are easy to lift and have separate reusable tops. Even when filled with books, they are light enough for most of the volunteers to move. They also flatten for easy storage when not in use.

Category Labels

You will need category labels to put on each end of your sorting boxes. These labels will be critical as you set up for your sale. As full boxes of books are unloaded from the trucks at your book sale site, they can be easily identified and placed at the appropriate sale table during your setup. Once you have selected the categories you will use, have a volunteer write or print labels for each category. Keep them in a convenient location in your sorting area, along with a supply of blank labels and markers in case you run out during a sorting session.

Tape

We recommend using packaging tape and tape dispensers to seal sorted boxes. Although it is not absolutely necessary to seal the boxes, they will be stored for months at a time and then transported to our sale site. The sealed boxes are much more secure, less apt to break open as they are moved, and keep books free from dust and creepy crawlers that may want to peruse or nibble on them.

Price Stickers

Self-adhesive, removable dots are useful for pricing some items (records, kids' board books, games, CDs, etc.). These dots can be purchased at almost any stationery store.

ARTS AND LITERATURE
Includes Drama and Poetry

Place these exceptions in the Collectible box:

Coffee-table (large-size) books
Modern Library
Movie editions of novels
First editions of famous authors
Edward Steichen, Ansel Adams, other
    prominent illustrators
Charles Dickens
Mark Twain

CHILDREN

Place these exceptions in the Collectible box:

Alice in Wonderland
Cherry Ames
Bobbsey Twins
Dick and Jane readers
Pop-up books
Shirley Temple

Put children's book sets on sets table.

Figure 2.2 🌐
Sample category signs.

Carts

Saving volunteers' backs needs to be a priority, so you will need some method for moving large numbers of books quickly and efficiently. Lancaster and Oro Valley have purchased or had donated several flatbed carts and book trucks for their sorting facilities. These are used to transport books from the sorting area to their storage area (in the same room, but books are heavy and they move six full boxes at a time). They also use the carts on book donation days, to bring books from the donors' cars into the facility and for removal of the discarded books (more on that sensitive topic in chapter 6). The Potsdam sale used a donated appliance dolly, and several volunteers brought other carts for use at the setup. A local bookstore chain was getting rid of some obsolete book trucks, and a Lancaster volunteer who works there part time got them for the warehouse.

Box Tally Sheets

Hang a tally sheet near the sorted box storage area where you can mark the category name of filled boxes before they are put in the storage area (fig. 2.3). It is important that all volunteers know how to properly inventory sorted boxes as they are placed in the storage area. An accurate count by category of all sorted books is essential for a smoothly run sale. Your sale layout and publicity committees will need this vital information. For mini sales, we have a separate tally sheet and a separate warehouse section to gather selected categories we want to sell at these smaller sales.

Ambiance

Ambiance—what an overused word! But there is something to be said for creating a pleasant atmosphere for your sorting and pricing workspace. Check with local carpet retailers for remnants that they might be willing to donate, especially if your facility has concrete floors. It will make such a difference to volunteers who stand in virtually the same place the entire time they are sorting or pricing books. Scour garage sales for a radio/CD player, a small refrigerator, a clock, and other amenities to make the place homey. A bulletin board not only gives a place to hang a scheduling calendar, it also serves as a spot for volunteer achievements, pictures, and other newsy items. Bring in colorful posters from the library or the local travel agency or movie theater to brighten things up. You might even try a few live plants!

Details from Our Sales

Lancaster

In Lancaster, we have two long rows of sorting tables. The volunteers sort between the two rows, turning around as needed to find the correct category. Unsorted books are in the middle of this area on their own table. Discard boxes are under all the tables, where sorters can throw musty, unsellable books. We use a clothesline tacked to wooden supports dropped from our high warehouse ceiling to hang our category signs. We also use this "laundry line" to attach special sorter's notes such as requests from the library and book club lists.

As much as possible, we schedule sorting times to accommodate our volunteer sorters. Wednesday mornings a group of volunteers who have become very close friends come and sort books. They sort for two hours, and often several of them then go out for lunch. This group also had a shower for a volunteer who recently adopted a baby from Guatemala, and they generally just like their sorting buddies, which include several male retirees. We also have a Sunday afternoon sorting time that is popular. Be sure to hang a calendar in the sorting room with the scheduled work times posted.

Potsdam

Potsdam's sorting room was set up in a U-shape, again with the category boxes placed on the tables alphabetically. Once priced, boxed, and tallied, the books were placed in the finished stacks after having been properly marked on the tally sheet. Sorting for Potsdam took place during the donation drop-off each week.

Oro Valley

We use a setup similar to Lancaster's with unsorted boxes in between two long rows of sorting tables. Because books are donated at our library and our warehouse, pricing is done at both sites. The books are then sorted, boxed, and stored at the warehouse.

Acquiring a facility that meets your needs will help your organization get a continual supply of donated books. Set up your workroom so that it is efficient and uses your space wisely. Be sure that you keep sufficient

BOX TALLY SHEET

Sale Spring 2004   Date 5/24/04

Category	Sorted Boxes	Total
$1.00 Paperbacks	///// ////	9
Arts & Literature	///// ///// ///// /	16
Biography	///// ///// //	12
Business/Law	///// /	6
Children	///// ///// ///// /////	20
Christmas	//	2
Computer Science	////	4
Foreign Language	///// ///	8
Gardening/Cookbooks	///// ///// ///	13
Hardback Novels	///// ///// ///// ///// ///// ///// ///// /	36
History/Politics	///// ///	8
Home Arts and Hobbies	///// //	7
Large Print	///	3
Light Romance	///// ///	8
Medicine/Health	///// //	6
Music	////	4
Mystery/Adventure	///// ///// ///// ///// ////	24
Newer Fiction	///// ///// ///// ///// ///// ///// //	32
Newer Nonfiction	///// ///// ///// ///// ///// ///	28
Oldies—Novels	///// ///// /	11
Paperback Novels	///// ///// ///// ///// ///// ///	28
Philosophy/Eastern Religion	////	4
Psychology/Sociology	///// ///// /	11
Records/Tapes/Videos	///// ///// /////	15
Reference/English	///// ////	9
Religion	///// ///// ///// /	16
Romance—Excl. Lt. Romance	///// ///// //	12

Science Fiction/Western	///// ////	9
Science/Nature	///// ///// ////	14
Sets/Encyclopedias	///// ///// ///// /	16
Signed by Author	////	4
Special-priced—Arts	///// ///// //	12
Special-priced—Children	///// ///// /	1
Special-priced—History	///// ///// ////	14
Special Priced—All Other	///// ///// /////	15
Sports/Humor	///// ////	9
Teens	///// /////	10
Textbooks	///// //	7
Travel/Geography	/////	5
	Total Boxes	478

Figure 2.3 [WEB]
Sample tally sheet for sorted boxes.

inventory of necessary supplies (a posted list of needed supplies is helpful) so sorting can continue uninterrupted. Schedule and communicate work times that are convenient for your volunteers. Making the facility a pleasant place to work will keep them coming back to sort and price books.

3

Directing the Show

The Book Sale Committee

 TIP

Have fun! The camaraderie outshines the hard work.

Initially you will have a small handful of volunteers for your book sale endeavors, but your volunteer base will grow quickly as you implement our recruiting ideas (chapter 4). Your committees can evolve as you have more volunteers to cover the diverse book sale activities.

Set up a book sale committee with interested Friends and other volunteers. A designated book sale chair or co-chairs will ensure that the book sale is represented by a united front. Having a central figure to field the inevitable questions and concerns is helpful for smooth operation of your project. The chair will need to understand the relationship between the Friends group and the library, and how the book sale project fits into the overall plans of each group. The book sale chair needs enough authority to be able to speak about the book sale to the community, to make decisions concerning the sale, and to have control over funds for initial startup costs. Additional subcommittees you may form will follow the basic work involved in preparing for the book sale, from sorting to pricing to sales and more. Each subcommittee will need a chairperson to bring their members together to discuss, plan, and do the work associated with the subcommittee. The flow and productivity of meetings, as well as the way members interact, are extremely important to keep volunteers enthused and engaged.

HOLDING PRODUCTIVE MEETINGS

As your book sale develops and volunteers are assigned specific responsibilities, it will be necessary to plan and implement the activities required for successful book sales.

You probably have been involved in meetings at work or in a volunteer group that were ineffective, boring, disorganized, or otherwise nonproductive. These types of meetings undermine the enthusiasm, fun, and efficiency of the organization. Following are some tips to help your organization hold productive, effective, and yes, even enjoyable meetings.

Carefully prepare a meeting agenda. Don't overload the agenda. Get input from committee people on agenda items. Invite attendees in writing if possible (e-mail is fine) and include a copy of the meeting agenda. Make sure the right people are invited to the meeting—committee members as well as guests who need to be informed of or otherwise contribute to the topics discussed. This advance agenda will give committee members a chance to think about the issues and come to the meeting prepared. Besides the topics to be discussed, the agenda should include the meeting place, starting time, and ending time.

Start the meeting on time, stick with the agenda as closely as possible, and either reach a decision on each item or assign responsibility for further action. Don't let the meeting drag on beyond the scheduled time. Meetings often become exciting with creative juices flowing, and good ideas stumble over each other wanting to be heard. These dynamics are what keep an organization vital and fun. On the other hand, you need to keep control of the meeting and learn to handle these creative outbursts, as well as any personal conflicts, in a productive and tactful manner. Experience is a wonderful teacher, but you can also learn many of these skills by observation. Most organizations employ at least one person who makes meeting management seem effortless; much can be learned from watching how that person handles difficult or boisterous situations without offending anyone or killing enthusiasm.

A minutes taker is helpful, especially regarding important decisions or votes. It is often a good idea for committee members to take turns preparing the minutes. If anyone is uncomfortable recording the minutes, don't insist.

Occasionally a pressing issue needs to be addressed, and you may need to table a less-pressing agenda item.

Be flexible, but save these rearrangements only for very important issues. Another option is to set up an ad hoc committee (a committee formed for a specific purpose) to research an item and report back to the full committee within a defined time frame.

Robert's Rules of Order can be followed for serious decision-making items, but an informal process is all that is really necessary. The key is to be sure that everyone is treated by all with mutual respect.

Details from Our Sales

Lancaster

Because we have been growing for fifty-seven years, we have a lot of volunteers who support our book sale efforts. Your sale may never want or need to get as big as the Lancaster sale. However, we want to share a vision that may help as you grow to meet your own needs. The book sale committee charts (figs. 3.1 and 3.2) will give you some ideas of committees you may want to set up for your book sale, with positions and responsibilities defined below. Most often, the chairs of the various subcommittees solicit and sign up volunteers to work with them on the subcommittee functions. Your sale will be unique, and your own committee positions will become evident to you based on the dynamics of your particular circumstances and group of volunteers.

Potsdam

The Potsdam book sale committee was made up of the entire Friends group. Because the small group was just getting established, everyone was called upon to assist in the book sale efforts. There was a book sale chair, and the president of the Friends was very involved and supportive of the book sale activities. The book sale project breathed new life and enthusiasm into the Friends group. Several subcommittees have since been created.

Oro Valley

In Oro Valley, the Friends board has established a permanent voting board position: the director of book sale operations. This director, appointed by the Friends board, reports book sale activities to the board but has autonomy to allow the book sale to function as a business, with experienced book sale volunteers making the day-to-day decisions. Although accountable

LANCASTER BOOK SALE COMMITTEE MEMBER TITLES AND RESPONSIBILITIES

Book Sale Chair
Responsible for overall activities of book sale committee

Approves all committee expenditures before submitting for payment

Liaison between book sale and Friends of the Library

Approves all publicity before release

Serves as spokesperson for sale

Appoints other committee members as needed

Book Sale Co-chair
Understudy for chair position. Assists chair where needed

Sorting Chair
Responsible for coordinating book sorting at the Book ReSort, including keeping accurate count by category of all sorted boxes ready for book sales

Schedules sorting sessions including assignment of volunteers in charge of sessions

Orders all sorting supplies

Works closely with warehouse manager to ensure smooth operating for box storage at warehouse

Responsible for key control and list of warehouse key-holders, subject to chair's approval

Pricing Chair
Sets up pricing sessions for rare and collectible books and oversees pricing of these books, including training sessions for new pricing committee volunteers

Maintains pricing lists for books frequently encountered to ensure consistency in pricing throughout the year

Electronics Chair
Responsible for sorting categorizing, and otherwise preparing electronic items for sale, including records, audiobooks, videotapes, CDs, and DVDs

Processing, pricing, and consulting with book sale chair for markdowns during book sale

Sets/Encyclopedias Chair
Pricing and packing all book sets—encyclopedias, cooking and gardening sets, literary sets, etc.— for book sales

Maintains detailed records of book pricing to ensure consistency and information on unsellable sets for future reference

Consults with book sale chair for sales markdowns during sale

Selling Chair
Responsible for recruiting and organizing volunteers to sell books during sales

Sets up tally and cashier tables at book sale, including written instructions for volunteers and all supplies needed at these tables

Prepares cashboxes each day of sale for cashiers

Collects, counts, and deposits proceeds from book sale, with a copy of each deposit slip given to library

Responsible for credit card machines used at sales, including reconciliation of signed customer receipts to daily settlement tapes run from machines

Keeps a record of all sales totals by day and by event, including historical information. Follows controls set for proper cash handling

Publicity Chair
Responsible for all media contacts concerning the book sales, working with chair and also library public relations director

Oversees printing and distribution of posters, bookmarks, and other printed matter

Reviews all press releases and printed matter with book sale chair before release

Warehouse Manager
Responsible for warehouse layout, book donations placement, sorted books pallet layout, and coordination of books removal for sales

Works closely with library maintenance staff for donation delivery and trash removal coordination

Helps at book donation drop-off the first Saturday of every month

Works with landlord and library staff to keep warehouse in good working condition

Coordinates removal and postsale return of all supplies used for book sales (includes conveyors, bookends, signs, and book trucks)

LANCASTER BOOK SALE COMMITTEE MEMBER TITLES AND RESPONSIBILITIES, *cont.*

Sign Committee

Duties include putting up necessary signs for all book sales. Includes new category signs as requested by chair and all miscellaneous signs as needed (arrows, Pay Here, Restrooms, etc.) at sales

Responsible for getting any new signs made. Takes down and files signs after sales

Sale Setup Chair

Helps book sale chair design sale layout

Coordinates materials required for the sale, including table rental and all supplies needed from warehouse

Contacts trucking company for book delivery

Oversees handling of books and unpacking on setup day

Spit 'n' Polish Chair

In charge of cleanup activities after sale

Arranges for unsold books to be removed and recruits volunteers to dismantle and remove tables

Restores facility to working order

Reviews disposition of unsold books with book sale chair

Hospitality Committee

Responsible for providing refreshments and lunch for sale setup core volunteers (about 30 people)

Works closely with book sale chair and setup chair to determine needs

Bookstore Managers (two year-round stores)

Coordinate volunteer schedule for Friends' used bookstores

Keep a list of emergency substitutes to ensure that store is always staffed

Advise sorting chair of book inventory needs for stores

Keep necessary supplies for efficient store operation

Oversee sales training, including customer relations, restocking, cash management, and credit card procedures

Internet Sales Chair

Trains and oversees volunteers assisting with online sales, including identifying books that are Web-worthy, setting appropriate prices, and posting clear, accurate descriptions and photos

Monitors bid cycle and packaging and oversees book shipment processes

Monitors PayPal account and follow-up correspondence and accounting

Figure 3.1 【WEB】

Sample roles and responsibilities for book sale committee members.

to the Friends board, the director of book sale operations needs this autonomy and continuity to function smoothly as the makeup of the board changes.

The basic structure of your book sale committee should fit your group's needs at any given point, depending on the dynamics of your sale and the makeup of your volunteers. Be flexible as you grow. One important factor to remember: train and develop your volunteers. This ensures a pool of volunteers who understand and know the details of how to run the book sale. Continuity and a succession plan, as successful businesses know, are important keys to future success.

ORO VALLEY BOOK SALE COMMITTEE MEMBER TITLES AND RESPONSIBILITIES

Director of Book Sale Operations

Oversees all aspects of book sale operations, including

- Two bookshops, working with managers
- Two annual book sales, working with co-chairs
- All book sale committees
- Volunteers (working with volunteer coordinator)
- Responsible for all keys and their distribution
- Reports to Friends board at monthly meetings

Book Sale Chair/Co-chair

Responsible for overseeing book sale

Serves as spokesperson for book sales

Produces floor layout plan

Assures volunteers are in place for every aspect of the sale, including setup and teardown

Assures publicity is in place

Arranges for unsold books disposition

Restores facility to working order

Arranges for stores to donate bags for bag day

Oversees setup and teardown, including lunch arrangements on full days

Oversees all money matters: counting of proceeds and record keeping by two people, and daily deposits

Completes training of volunteers on cash registers prior to sale days

Publicity Chair

Responsible for all media contacts (working with book sale chairs)

Oversees printing of posters, bookmarks, and other printed matter

Reviews all press releases and printed matter with director and book sale chairs before release

Sorting Chair

Oversees sorting operation, making sure filled boxes are tallied for floor layout plan

Assures books are sorted and boxed in timely manner

Oversees volunteer schedule

Assures sort stays neat and clean

Keeps necessary supplies available

Maintains supply of computer-generated box labels

Pricing Chair

Oversees continuing pricer training

Hold occasional meetings to keep pricing consistent

Assures books are priced in timely manner

Warehouse Chair

Responsible for warehouse layout

Coordinates books removal for sale

Oversees warehouse maintenance

Responsible for computers and other office/warehouse equipment

Volunteer Coordinator

Schedules and trains volunteers as needed

Book Shoppe Manager (one per store)

Coordinates schedule with volunteer coordinator, keeping all sales shifts covered

Oversees sales training of new volunteers

Keeps shop neat and clean

Originates displays and occasional special sales

Keeps inventory fresh and oversees monthly inventory control, usually pulling books over three months old and replacing with new stock

Trains volunteers to keep shelves filled

Works with director of book sale operations to assure shops are running well, keeping continuity in pricing and management policies

Internet Sales Chair

Researches items to determine suitability for online selling

Trains and oversees other researchers

Enters book data online and trains others to do so

Oversees packaging and shipping of sold books

Monitors sales sites and handles correspondence with buyers and sales sites

Monitors PayPal account

Figure 3.2

Sample roles and responsibilities for book sale committee members.

4

Casting Call
How to Get and Keep Volunteers

 TIP

Praise and celebrate your volunteers!

A book sale requires a constant supply of donated books and a suitable place to sort them. But it also requires volunteers. Lots of volunteers! Only a few people are needed initially to begin book sale activities, because one of the first functions of your book sale committee will be to solicit workers. Libraries have the most wonderful dedicated volunteers—you just need to give them the opportunity to help the library with the book sale project.

HOW TO SOLICIT VOLUNTEERS

First, you will need several people to agree to work on committees to run the book sale (see chapter 3). Later you'll also need a number of book sorters/pricers as well as people for other positions. Families, friends, and general word of mouth are great ways to begin growing your pool of volunteers. Beyond your immediate circle, however, there is a whole community waiting to be tapped. As your sale continues to grow and as volunteers move away or become busy with raising small children or other responsibilities, you will need more help. Lancaster found themselves in this situation and advertised in the local newspaper (fig. 4.1). They had an overwhelming response.

Many of the new volunteers had been customers of the Lancaster book sales, some were new to the community and wanted to get involved, and others were just curious. Learning to sort and price books was the main interest of this new group of volunteers. The book sale committee subsequently held four very well-attended training sessions with the new volunteers.

If you have attended other book sales, you probably noticed that the majority of workers are female, many of advanced age. We don't mean to be politically incorrect, but for the running of your book sale and its viability for the future, this prevalent structure has to change. A varied mix of both age and gender in your pool of volunteers can bring new perspective to your book sale project. Don't be shy about asking younger folks as well as husbands, boyfriends, brothers, and sons to become part of the book sale team. Try holding a wine-and-cheese sorting session, inviting couples to come and see the warehouse operation. When donors bring book donations to your facility, offer to show them your book processing operation—especially if current volunteers are present, enjoying themselves while helping raise money for the library. By following these methods, Lancaster now has nearly as many male as female volunteers, some of them husband-and-wife teams. The average age of the group has dropped from 60s to late 40s.

Maintain a spreadsheet of your book sale volunteers, including name, address, phone numbers, e-mail address, and their specific volunteer activities. This record will be useful for many reasons, including contact information for book sale volunteers, thank-you notes, and meetings.

Consider requiring each new volunteer to fill out and sign a volunteer application (fig. 4.2), including a conflict of interest section for those who may already sell books, whether at a brick-and-mortar bookshop or online. (See "Volunteer Issues," below.) A verbal noncompete policy may be sufficient—asking all new volunteers up front if they are booksellers. If the answer is yes, point them toward other volunteer opportunities, such as shelving or otherwise helping out in the library.

HOW TO KEEP VOLUNTEERS

Until your new volunteers become as insanely dedicated and addicted to book sale activities as you are, you will need to pay attention to them. Make sure they feel involved and part of the book sale team. There are many

---

FROM: Jane Doe, Publicity Chair
SUBJECT: Lancaster Public Library Book Sale Seeking Volunteers
DATE: March 15, 2000

FOR IMMEDIATE RELEASE
Volunteers are being sought to help with the annual book sale sponsored by the Friends of the Lancaster Public Library. There are many opportunities to get involved and bring new ideas and energy to the sale.

A general book sale planning session will be at the Lancaster Public Library on Tuesday, April 20, from 10 to 11 a.m., with a repeat session on Wednesday, April 28, from 7 to 8 p.m. The sessions will focus on basics of the book sale and how volunteers can build upon the last 46 successful years. Each session will cover the same information.

Volunteers are needed particularly to help sort the donated books throughout the year. A training session for sorting will be held on Monday, May 17, from 10 a.m. to noon at the Book ReSort at 630 Janet Avenue, Lancaster. There will be a repeat session from 7 to 9 that evening. Space is limited for the training sessions.

Figure 4.1 WEB
Sample volunteer press release. Press releases should be printed on official Friends or Library letterhead.

diverse activities involved with a book sale, so try to match up their interests with the jobs that need to be done. The publicity function could use special writing and public relations skills. Computer skills are a big plus for reports, volunteer lists, and signs requiring graphics. Music and film buffs can help sort and price sheet music, CDs, DVDs, videos, and records. (Yes, vinyl records still sell!) Internet expertise is helpful for online book sales. The list is endless.

Lancaster has a warehouse manager who does not want to sort or sell books but is a genius at keeping the warehouse functioning smoothly, considering the volume of books and other equipment stored there. Having a warehouse manager frees up the other volunteers to focus on the books. Two other Lancaster volunteers take care of signs for the various sales, including getting them laminated, putting the signs up at each sale, taking them down and neatly storing them after each sale and making new signs as needed. What gems they are—and they take immense pride in doing a good job. Lancaster has had many positive comments about the terrific signage at the book sales, and the credit goes to the sign committee.

The secret is to try to match the volunteer to the job, looking at skill, temperament, personality, and compatibility when paired with another volunteer—all those things that will help volunteers engage in an assigned task and have fun while doing it. A few appreciative comments from book sale leadership also let volunteers know they are making a difference. A personal phone call to invite volunteers to come and sort with you will keep them interested. Thank-you notes for a job well done are also helpful and appreciated. All these personal contacts will make your volunteers feel welcome and needed.

Sorting books all year long is the most labor-intensive function of the book sale, and we do offer incentives to volunteers. They may purchase books (at regular sale prices) as they sort and price (another volunteer must price the book for them). This is great for people who love to read—have you checked out bookstore prices lately? Also, many of our donated books are out of print, so they aren't even available in most bookstores. We also offer flexible volunteer hours, perfect for busy people. Some of our volunteers head to warmer climates for the winter (or cooler climates for the summer), and others may like to travel a lot. They are welcomed back when they are available; they can stay away for weeks or months at a time without feeling guilty or unhelp-

TIP
Keep the working atmosphere enjoyable and friendly so everyone will look forward to being there.

ful. Of course, some sale functions carry time-sensitive responsibilities, but those are defined up front to volunteers who are willing to take on those tasks.

Details from Our Sales

Lancaster

Lancaster's book sale runs smoothly (mostly!) in large part because of the volunteers who help us year after year. We have a book sale chair, and in most years a co-chair who is learning from and being mentored by the chair. Our book sale committees have several dozen people doing various functions throughout the year. Although we started out on a much smaller scale, our early book sale successes and our good recruiting methods brought us more and more volunteers.

Assisting the book sale committee are literally hundreds of volunteers. Absolutely no book dealers or sellers are allowed to be on the book sale committee or help with sorting, selling, or setup. We know some book sales allow this, but we feel it truly is a conflict of interest. You put both the sale and the volunteer in an awkward position, and it is best avoided.

Sorting and pricing books are the most labor-intensive activities for our book sale. In earlier days, the sorting and pricing were done a few weeks before the sale. Now we sort books and price collectible books all year long. Sorting is a huge effort for us—and the most fun. We sort about 3,000 boxes into many categories for our big spring sale and about 600 more boxes for our mini sales. In addition we keep our two used bookstores supplied with books all year long.

There is also a need for volunteers to set up for the spring sale, many more to run the sale, and still more to clean up after the sale. You will find a dedicated core in your organization to assist in most aspects of the book sale, from sorting to cleanup. We have a large group of volunteers who take selling shifts and other functions during the big spring sale, but we do solicit volunteers from the community for setup day. Hundreds come out

FRIENDS OF THE ORO VALLEY PUBLIC LIBRARY BOOK SHOPPE/ BOOK SALE VOLUNTEER APPLICATION

(Please Print)

Name _____

Address _____ Zip _____

Home phone _____ Cell phone _____

E-mail address _____

Are you a full-time resident? yes / no   If not, when will you be available to work? _____

☐ Check here if you are under 18 years of age.

Emergency Contact

Name _____ Relationship _____

Home phone _____ Cell phone _____

Book Shoppe Volunteers
- Must learn to operate the cash register, make change, count money before and after a shift.
- May be required to lift, bend, and reach to stock shelves and receive book donations.
- Must be able to take phone messages.
- Must be able to work 3.5-hour shifts.
- Must be able to interact comfortably with patrons.

What days and times are you available to work in the Shoppe? (Check all that apply)

☐ Monday 9:45–1:00	☐ Wednesday 9:45–1:00	☐ Friday 9:45–1:00
☐ Monday 12:45–4:15	☐ Wednesday 12:45–4:15	☐ Friday 12:45–4:15
☐ Tuesday 11:45–3:00	☐ Thursday 11:45–3:00	☐ Saturday 9:45–1:00
☐ Tuesday 2:45–5:15	☐ Thursday 2:45–5:15	☐ Saturday 12:45–4:15

Semiannual Book Sale Volunteers
- Must be able to tally sales and give change.
- May be required to lift, bend, and reach to stock shelves and tables.
- Must be able to work 3-hour shifts.

Would you like to be contacted to work at the: ☐ Spring Book Sale   ☐ Fall Book Sale

Persons who sell books may present a conflict of interest to our book operations.

Do you currently sell books? yes / no

This information is correct at the time of this signing:

_____

Signature   Date

(FOR FOVPL USE ONLY)

Interviewer _____ Date _____

Areas of interest _____

_____

Comments _____

_____

Figure 4.2 WEB
Sample volunteer application.

to help, knowing the project benefits the library and the community.

Potsdam

Because of the expertise Lancaster provided, the Potsdam sale grew very quickly, which presented them with the immediate need to recruit volunteers. They were a small group (six members) and were planning a big sale—20,000 books! They called friends, family, neighbors, and coworkers. Volunteers were eager to support the library. By holding a very successful first sale, they now have a growing list of volunteers to call upon.

Potsdam was following up on a Lancaster suggestion: to be adopted as a special project by a local service organization—such as Rotary, Optimists, or Kiwanis—to assist in specific areas such as sale setup, selling at the sales, and transporting books to and from the sale. The local newspaper also has a "Volunteers Needed" column where Potsdam has asked for help. When the schools are in session, they get help from college fraternities, sororities, and high school students.

Oro Valley

Oro Valley has book sale co-chairs who divide up the tasks and responsibilities. The year 2011 marked the ninth year for our two annual sales, and most volunteers return enthusiastically to work both sales.

We recently held a "Volunteers Requested" coffee-and-refreshments session in the library, which we had advertised in the local paper. Several veteran volunteers spoke briefly about book sale opportunities. It was a very informal and relaxed session, and nearly all those attending have since become volunteers.

A few cautions as your book sale develops: Rapid growth can be a little scary. Be flexible as you learn how to best run your sale. You will find that your volunteers will be supportive as you learn from your mistakes in the beginning days of your project. Until you get to know your volunteers' skills, you will surely not have all the right people doing the right tasks. You may also frustrate volunteers as you make on-the-spot decisions for unanticipated problems that arise. Keeping volunteers informed is important in your growth period. Organization will improve as you move forward.

VOLUNTEER ISSUES

Volunteers will be a key and vital resource for your sale. You need to nurture, praise, and keep these volunteers coming back. Set simple rules and guidelines, but know that on occasion you will need to be firm and forthright to handle certain situations. Below are a few examples of some issues our chairs have had to deal with over the course of time. These problems have been a very small part of our glorious adventures with our volunteers, so don't be discouraged. Just be aware that situations will occasionally arise that you will need to address. Take care of any issues quickly so that you keep a happy and cohesive group of volunteers.

The Noncompete Clause

You must be very careful to not allow book dealers or other booksellers to be part of your volunteer group. Because they are in the book business, there is a direct conflict of interest. Before you accept volunteers, ask the question "Do you sell books?" See Oro Valley's noncompete agreement (fig. 4.3) for an example of a formal statement to this effect. Also, if one of your volunteers is buying a huge amount of books from your sorting activity, be aware and have an open discussion with them about it.

Buying Perks

Our volunteers are allowed to buy books throughout the year as a perk for working. Be sure that your volunteers pay for their books as they leave.

Reliability

The book sale organization needs to be able to count on volunteers to follow through on their commitment to the book sale. Occasionally you will have to deal with procrastinators or people who don't show up at all. Usually a gentle reminder is enough, but sometimes you may have the wrong person in a critical job. Be alert to these issues, and you will soon learn which volunteers are the most reliable.

Behavior

On the rare occasion when a volunteer becomes disruptive or overbearing, or exhibits otherwise unacceptable behavior, you will need to have a discussion with them and quickly resolve the issue.

SPECIAL SKILLS VOLUNTEERS

A solid base of volunteers is necessary for a successful book sale. Just like any other group, the diversity of talents within your organization can be a truly valuable resource for your book sale. Listed below are a few ways our book sales have used the special skills of our volunteers. The volunteers are usually thrilled to see their talents recognized and put to use, and your book sale reaps the benefits.

Details from Our Sales

Lancaster

Lancaster has such a broad base of volunteers that we can use our people in special ways that you may not be able to until you grow your pool of volunteers.

VOLUNTEER NONCOMPETE AGREEMENT WITH THE FRIENDS OF THE ORO VALLEY PUBLIC LIBRARY

In consideration of the trust and responsibility inherent in my position as a volunteer in any capacity in the Book Operations Area of the Friends of the Oro Valley Public Library (FOVPL):

I, the undersigned, hereby agree that I shall not compete with the book selling efforts of the FOVPL by using my accessibility to donated books, whether for sale to the general public or available for later sales, to buy and resell these books for my own personal financial gain.

This agreement terminates when I am no longer a volunteer in the Book Operations Area of the Friends of the Oro Valley Library.

Signed: _____

Date: _____

Figure 4.3 WEB
Sample volunteer noncompete agreement.

However, we want to get you thinking about some of the imaginative ways our group has recognized special talents of our volunteers and kept them eager to help. Here are a few examples of how we have tapped into volunteer talent.

Lancaster has a publicity chair who thrives on her book sale job. She has made and nurtured contact with our local newspapers and television stations, developing relationships that make the reporters supportive of our fund-raising efforts. We get great publicity because of her diligence. The media know they can count on her to provide concrete, creative information that they can use for interesting angles about our sale. She has mailed flyers and sent e-mail to libraries in surrounding counties and has expanded outreach advertising within our community through many online sources for radio, TV, and newspapers, as well as Facebook and YouTube.

The boxes of sorted books are marked on each end with a category label. These labeled boxes can then be put on the appropriate tables at our setup in preparation for unpacking the boxes. We used to handwrite these labels, but now we have a volunteer who makes printed labels for us. As the boxes fly off conveyors and carts at our sale setup, these printed labels are so much easier to read. The category labels used to be kept in a flat box at the end of the sorting tables, where they were rifled through to find the label needed. A handyman-type volunteer made a wooden box for the labels to stand up in, with separators between each category. Now sorters can quickly find the labels they need.

A local optometrist and book sale volunteer offered to help us sort and price our growing collection of donated records. He worked as a disc jockey in college and had also started a local record club in our area. This club draws record aficionados from a five-state area. Our volunteer has a lot of expertise in this neglected part of our sale. He has brought in two friends who help to organize and price our records. They have an old record player in their work corner, and music can be heard as they go about their tasks. Our sales in the records area have quadrupled since we have these three volunteers cleaning, sorting, and fairly pricing these records. They also advertise our sale to their record club members, which may account for some of the increased revenue.

In the other electronics areas of our sale, we have two volunteers who price and sort CDs, videos, audiobooks, and DVDs. One of the volunteers is a retired computer analyst who also plays drums in a local jazz band, and the other is a retired RCA engineer. The caliber of our offerings in this segment of our sale has improved a hundredfold. These two fellows have a great time as they go about their volunteer jobs of cleaning, weeding out the "junk," and researching items on the Internet. Their expertise and growing knowledge in these genres have increased interest in these areas of our sale. This year we offered about 5,000 DVDs, CDs, VHS tapes, and audiobooks, all having been individually scrutinized and priced by these two volunteers. They also are active floor workers at the sale, artfully marketing their wares with great signage and location and acting as personal shoppers for our sale customers. Their diligence and hard work add so much to our sale success, and they have great fun doing it.

Potsdam

At their first big sale, Potsdam decided they would like to have some special activities during the sale to draw more interest. One of their volunteers taught customers how to make bookmarks that looked like a lovely Japanese woman in a kimono and sash. The volunteer also orchestrated a group from the local college who would write your name on a bookmark in four different languages. What a hit these were at the sale, adding to Potsdam's success. A local high school student acted out a humorous Japanese story that kept the onlookers laughing.

One volunteer made printed category signs for the sorting site as well as the sale. Another volunteer made wooden sign holders so the signs would be more visible at the sale. Potsdam's library director, formerly a children's librarian, was an invaluable source in helping set up the children's and teen books at the sale.

Oro Valley

Oro Valley has discovered several computer-literate volunteers. One of them creates great signs with terrific graphics and also has re-created the layout of our sales floor so we can hand out printed maps to customers. Another volunteer has turned the online books sales into an extremely profitable venture and also is training others in that process. This training of others is critical: as some volunteers leave to pursue other interests, there are others trained to step up and take over.

As with Lancaster, Oro Valley has a great volunteer who has made valuable contact with the media. She also produces our world-class newsletter.

Libraries are a magnet for volunteers. Begin with a small core group to help organize your efforts, then reach out to your community for individuals to support your book sale.

Match your new volunteers' skills to the tasks to be performed. Get to know your volunteers so you can use them to everyone's best advantage. Often a casual conversation with a volunteer will lead to a delightful discovery of talents that will enhance your book sale and your volunteer's esteem and usefulness. Let your volunteers know they are making a difference for your library and that they are part of a team.

5

Production
Categorizing and Organizing Book Donations

 TIP

Start out with fewer rather than more categories. Keep it simple until you master the basic mechanics of sorting books

Sorting is the key to building a successful sale. Make the sorting training fun—it is not a big deal if a book is in a wrong category, as long as it gets to the sale. Sometimes you will have different opinions as to category—does a biography on Babe Ruth go in Sports or in the Biography category? Somehow it doesn't matter, and your customers may find some in each category. Set out some basic rules, particularly about higher-priced books, and then let your volunteers loose. Sorting books, in our opinion, is the most fun part of your book sale project!

Selecting book sorting categories appropriate for your book sale is a major start-up consideration. There are as many variations of category setups as there are book sales. Everyone does it differently, and you will need to determine what best suits your sale. We will give you some ideas to help your decision, but ultimately you will need to settle on a category mix that fits your own needs. Set up training sessions as soon as you feel comfortable with the process you have in place.

CONSIDERATIONS AS YOU DEVELOP SORTING CATEGORIES

Space Limitations

More categories mean more individual space for each segment you separately handle for sorting as well as selling.

Pricing Policies

As you discuss your category mix, you will need to make decisions about the price ranges for your books. Many book sales set basic low-end prices for hardback as well as paperback books. Then they determine what groups of books will be priced higher than the base price. Some price points and specially priced book groups above your basic price will require a specific category—for example, Current Fiction. In chapter 6, we give you detailed information on pricing structure, which may be helpful as you outline your own policy.

To Add or Not to Add, That Is the Question!

Everyone, including your volunteers, has a certain niche of books they would like to see have a special category. Avoid outside pressure to add categories that may not be in the best interest of your sale. You will learn from customer comments and suggestions during and after your book sales what categories they would like to see at your book sale. You will not always be able to, nor always want to, meet their requests. For example, if you have 100,000 books offered for sale, you probably cannot meet a request to put them alphabetically by author, as suggested at the Lancaster sale . . .

Special Categories

Some geographic areas reflect a different eclectic or intellectual bent. You may want to accommodate these interests by setting up select categories that meet local needs. As an example, in Lancaster there is a great interest in religious books. Lancaster is a very religiously diverse community and one with strong ecumenical bonds. Because the Friends get so many donations of religious books, Philosophy and Eastern Religions have been put into a separate category. This may not be necessary or desirable in your own area. Also

in Lancaster, because donations and the sale are on such a huge scale, Autographed Books is a separate category. In Potsdam, with two local colleges and two more colleges in the next town, an Education category has proved to be popular. A Southwest category works well in Oro Valley.

Some books are so unique that they defy categorization. Do not be tempted to set up categories to satisfy these unusual items. Simply put them in the category closest to their definition, and do not lose any sleep over a book that may not be exactly in the right place. Get the price points right, and leave the category worries behind you. Your customers will find the books, and some of them actually get a kick out of finding sorting flub-ups, such as *The Vitamin Bible* in the Religion category.

Details from Our Sales

Lancaster

Our Lancaster sale has settled on—for now—39 different categories for sorting books! It is a cumbersome number and requires a lot of space for sorting as well as book sale layout. This large number of categories has developed over a span of 57 years, but for the last ten years we have only tweaked it a bit, mostly to update category names rather than change the substance. For example, the old Psychology/Sociology category has been changed to Self-Help. We recently changed the Children and Teen books into *three* categories: Children, Early Readers (from first to sixth grade), and Young Adults (seventh grade and up). The response was very positive from our shoppers, and we got more older kids looking in the Young Adult section since we upgraded the age group there.

Arts & Literature
Autographed
Biography
Business
Children
Christmas
Computer
Cookbooks
Crafts & Hobbies

Early Readers
Foreign Language
Gardening
Hardback Novels 1970–2003
History/Politics
Large Print
Light Romance—Harlequin/Silhouette ($2 per small plastic bagful)
Medicine & Health
Music—sheet music & music books
Mystery—HB & PB
Newer Fiction—2003 and newer
Newer Nonfiction—2003 and newer
Oldies Fiction—pre-1970
Paperback Fiction
Philosophy
Psychology & Self-Help
Records/DVDs/CDs/Audiobooks
Reference & English
Religion
Romance
Science/Nature
Sci-Fi/Westerns
Sets (any books with volumes—encyclopedias, children's sets, history, crafts, etc.)
Special-priced Books—History, Arts & Lit, Child/ Teen, General Sports, Humor
Textbooks
Travel
Young Adult

Potsdam

Potsdam started out with just a few categories: Hardback Fiction, Paperback Fiction, Hardback Nonfiction, Paperback Nonfiction, Children's, and a few others. They soon added many more categories to accommodate the diversity of books being donated. Potsdam, though on a much smaller scale, now has nearly as many categories as Lancaster. This made sorting decisions easier, and their first sale's success, with many positive customer comments, told Potsdam they were on a good track.

Oro Valley

Oro Valley pricers not only price each book, but they determine its category and write that inside the book. The books are then transported to the sorting facility, where volunteers put them in the correct category box. Here are the list of categories that work well for us:

Arts and Literature
Biography
Business
Children
Collectible/Rare
Computer
Cooking
Crafts and Home Arts
Entertainment/DVD/VHS/CD/Music Books/ Audiobooks
Fiction
Fiction paperback
Foreign Language
Gardening
Health
History
Large Print
Mystery
Mystery paperback
Nature and Science
Politics
Reference
Religion
Romance
Science Fiction
Self Help
Sets
Southwest
Sports, Games and Humor
Travel
Western
Young Adult

HOW TO SORT

On to the sorting! Set up organized sorts for the volunteers with a knowledgeable volunteer in charge of the sorting session. It is fun to sort as a group, and the sorting group will all learn as questions are asked and answered. Create your own version of Keys to Sorting Books (fig. 5.1) and keep the document available in the sorting room. New sorters should also read any helpful hints on your category signs. Provide copies of the

Collectible Books list (appendix C), which includes items that can command higher prices and should be set aside for research or for special pricing.

HOW TO TRAIN YOUR SORTERS

Training your book sorters well is a real key to success. Knowing how to sort books into the appropriate categories is important, but the most critical thing your sorters must learn is how to recognize and separate the books that command premium prices. The majority of your books will sell for your base price (Lancaster's base price is $2 for adult hardbacks, $1 for children's hardbacks, and 50 cents for all paperbacks). Yet there are many books that can and should sell for much more. Precise sorting will make the difference between ho-hum and blockbuster sales for your organization.

Gather a small group of new volunteers. Six or eight people are probably all you will want to train at a time. One-on-one training, of course, is always good, but in the beginning you may want to give everyone a crash course. Use Keys to Sorting Books (figure 5.1) as a guide; also use the Collectibles listing in appendix C. It is a good idea to make a copy for each trainee to keep. It is a lot of information to absorb at one time, and they will be able to keep the lists for reference.

Lancaster stresses the importance of identifying the books that can be sold for more than the basic price. If a book belongs in the Rare box or should be specially priced then there is no need even to consider identifying a category. So the first important thing is *price*.

The second point to consider is *condition*. The book should be scrutinized (flipping through each page from back to front only takes a few seconds) for torn or missing pages, water damage, and also any treasures, including money, that the previous owner left for you. Any found treasures, of course, belong to the book sale. At Lancaster last year, a sorter found $20 and $50 bills in an old Russian grammar book that amounted to $620! If you are lucky, the author might have signed the book. If you are very unlucky, someone may have cut out the guts of the book to make a secret hiding place. Or you may find silverfish hiding—they love paper!

Once the price point and condition have been determined, if you now are holding a base-price book that is sellable, you need to decide in which basic price category it fits. Setting up your sorting room categories alphabetically, as we suggested earlier, is very helpful

TIP

New sorters are often happy to have settled on a category for a particular book and often fail to remember or recognize that it should be at a higher price point. Be sure that experienced sorters are involved in the sort and watching for these missteps by inexperienced volunteers.

here. Having some basic notes on the category signs helps to answer a lot of questions in sorters' minds. See the Category Sign Samples for a few ideas. For example, we determined those Diet Books—we get a lot of them—should be included in our Medicine and Health category, and we have noted this on the Medicine and Health category sign. This type of notation helps everyone to be consistent.

Lancaster conducts training sessions several times throughout the year for new sorters. As we get one or two new volunteers, they get some individual attention from one of our premier sorters. Potsdam and Oro Valley train as needed, also using one-on-one assistance from experienced volunteers.

Sorting training is critical, and even though you may not feel like an expert yet, you know more than the new volunteers do. You will all learn as you go and will be surprised at how quickly the basics can be mastered. If you sort and price books often, you will always learn new things as your fellow volunteers talk and discuss books throughout the work session. That is one of the joys of volunteering!

BOOK DISCARDS AND DISPOSAL ISSUES

One of the toughest issues you will face is the decision to throw some books out. Not all books are in sellable condition. Many donated books have missing covers, broken spines, are mildewed, or are in otherwise deplorable condition. Do not—we repeat—*do not* take these books to your sale. We are successful in our sales because of the quality of the books we present for sale. You will get a well-deserved reputation for the caliber of your sale if you learn to do the unspeakable—throw out the books that are in bad condition. This does not apply to the few Rare/Collectible books that are highly sought. A Gutenberg Bible in any shape is a gold mine.

KEYS TO SORTING BOOKS

Sorting

1. Select a book and check its condition. Discard the book if
   - the cover is missing.
   - the book is profusely written in or is heavily highlighted, other than inscriptions.
   - the book is dirty soiled or mildewed. Mildew will spread to other books.
   - there are torn, missing, or loose pages, unless it's a very valuable book.

2. Check book for the following:
   - Date published
   - Author's or illustrator's signature
   - First edition of a very popular author
   - Interesting illustrations or bookplates

3. Select a category
   In this order, consider if book is suitable for the following categories:
   - Rare/Collectible (learn to review the alphabetical listing). Include gardening and cookbooks that are good quality. Lancaster sets these books aside to be priced by Pricing Committee.
   - Newer Fiction and Nonfiction (less than 6 years old) will be priced anywhere from $3 to $8. (See chapter 6 for details.)
   - Autographed Books—set aside for Pricing Committee.
   - Book Sets—place these in the "Sets" area for pricing by others.
   - If none of the above applies, then find the most suitable subject category. Check category signs for help, and ask any questions of the person in charge of the sort session.

Preparing Sorting Boxes

1. Place appropriate labels on both ends of box.
2. Pack books solidly, tape the top closed when box is full, and place box on cart.
3. When cart is full, mark tally sheet and stack boxes in "Sorted" area. It is very important to mark tally sheet as boxes move to the completed area, as this count by category will be the basis for the sale layout.

Objects Found in Books

All objects found in books are book sale property. Any money found should be given to the Sorting Chair for delivery to the Selling Committee. Other interesting "treasures" found should be placed in the Treasures Box in the sorting room.

Purchase of Books by Volunteers

As a reward for helping to sort books, sorters and pricers may purchase books from the work area. The book prices for volunteers are the same as the regular book sale price. If the book is a Rare/Collectible item, the sorter puts his name and phone number on a slip inside the book and leaves it for the pricing committee. When the book is priced, the volunteer will be called and can decide at that time if they want the book at that price.

Sign Out by Sorters

Sorters sign a volunteer time sheet with their name, the date, and the hours they spent sorting. This helps us to tally our volunteer hours. This information is also helpful if a volunteer has left behind any personal items, such as a jacket or hat. The sign-in sheet will show who was at the work session.

Figure 5.1 WEB
Sample book sorting procedure.

Train Your Sorters and Pricers to Open the Books and Check the Quality

Part of the training for your volunteers will be teaching them about book condition. A book needs to be examined for unseemly marking, massive highlighting, torn or missing pages, and so on. During this examination, treasures (including money) may also be discovered. A thorough examination of each book is a must—looking for autographs, publication dates, and

TIP

Set up a preliminary listing of the categories you think will be appropriate for your sale. Be sure that your sorters and pricers know what books should be included in each category.

---

the like—and certainly required for making a decision about the book's condition. Books by highly desirable authors, such a Stephen King or John Updike, can be a little shabby and still sell. But other run-of-the-mill books you see by the dozens should be in good condition or need to be discarded.

Weeding Out the Undesirable Books Leaves More Room for the Good Stuff!

The hardest job for our volunteers—people who very likely love books—is to discard books. It just goes against some principle that says, "Gee, *someone* could read this book." Our organization's goal is to sell books cheaply and to make a lot of money for the library. Along the way, we donate books to many kinds of local agencies, and we offer some leftovers from the sale to nonprofit organizations. But in order to become very successful at this sale business, you will need to discard some categories freely. There are only so many hardback novels by Frank Yerby that you can sell. Your discard decision will become easier as you get more donations. In the beginning, maybe you will keep most of the books you receive. Just remember to put your best foot forward at the sale. Remove Sale and Bargain stickers from books, wipe them off if they are dusty, and make your books look as presentable as possible.

Lancaster is lucky enough to have had a local book authority help price their Rare/Collectible books in the past. He trained the other volunteers well, and they are pretty good at spotting the rare books as opposed to a mere Golden Oldie that sells for $2. Potsdam also had a very reputable local book dealer who helped with the pricing. Lancaster, Potsdam, and Oro Valley all use the Internet as a resource (see appendix D, "Internet Resources"). You will learn some of the rare/collectible recognition the hard way, and you just might discard books that are worth a lot of money. When in doubt, have a volunteer research the book online, or find a local book dealer you can trust to help you price your

rare finds. A general rule of thumb would be to keep any books printed before 1900. This is such a generalization that it is not very useful, but it is a starting point regarding books to research. The Collectible Books list in appendix A will give you a good idea of some desirable collectible books, and you will want to expand this list as you learn more.

Discard Books Discreetly

The public does not want to know that you throw books out! Although we are not hiding the fact that we discard books during the sorting process, there are some cautions. If someone brings you ten boxes of donated books you can use and a box of old encyclopedias that you do not want, at least wait until they are out of the parking lot before you put the unwanted set in the recycling bin. We are careful not to blatantly throw out books. Many people will not understand. Lancaster had a woman threaten to run over the library director because of discarded books. The woman said, "These books could be used in Africa or some Third World country." The director explained the prohibitive transportation costs and suggested a large donation from the woman might help. No money was forthcoming, of course. Just be discreet as you do the necessary weeding of unsellable books.

There will be some books that need to be trashed—books that have been stored in wet basements or bird-infested attics. Do not ruin the wonderful books you are keeping by packing theses undesirable books with them.

Using our guidelines, carefully consider and select those categories appropriate for your book sale. Clearly define to your volunteers the types of books that will be included in each of your selected categories. This will eliminate questions and make your categorizing more uniform.

Our Keys to Sorting Books will guide you through productive and enjoyable work sessions. Training your volunteers to diligently use Keys to Sorting Books will result in consistently higher sales.

Discards are a normal by-product of your sorting process. Keep the quality of your book sale high by helping your volunteers understand the reasons that some books must be discarded. Make suitable arrangements for removal of your discards and your leftover sale books.

6

Ticket Price

What to Charge for Books and Electronic Media

Book sale prices vary immensely. We'll give you some guidelines and information about our pricing techniques, but your group will need to discuss and agree on how you will price your books.

In Lancaster we have set a base price for adult hardbacks at $2, Children's and Young Adult hardbacks at $1, and the base price for all paperbacks at 50 cents. (We just raised the hardback base price to $2 after 12 years of selling the hardbacks for $1 each.) Our base prices are very reasonable, as we like to give the general readers in our community a good deal and we want to sell as many books as we can cheaply. These base-price books make up about half the volume of our sale. They do *not*, however, make up half our profits!

The base-price books are not priced inside each book. Instead, we separate our sale into two sections—base-priced and individually priced books. This technique cuts in half the time and effort of individually pricing each book. Our big spring sale has over 250,000 books for sale. Signs noting the base price are scattered throughout this unpriced section, and the individually priced section has many signs telling shoppers that each book is priced inside the front cover. This process has worked very well for years.

Listed below are the price points for the specially priced categories of books.

NEWER FICTION BOOKS

Books in this category are no more than six or seven years old and are in very good condition. We sell lots of good-quality current paperbacks at $1 each. These books are those published in the last six or seven years. These are the *mass-market* paperbacks (regular small size—about 4-by-6 3/4 inches) as opposed to the larger *trade* paperbacks, which are about 5½-by-8¼ inches. We price the trade paperbacks at $2 to $4 depending on the book. Check the publisher's prices often listed on the back of the book or the spine. Many of these books sell for $14 to $16 when new, and you can use a rule-of-thumb of pricing the book no more than one-quarter of the publisher's price. We pencil the price *lightly* on the first page on the upper right-hand corner, or on the second page if the first page is a dark color. If many of the first pages are dark, put the price on a pricing dot on the front cover—we do this with a pen rather than a pencil. *Never* write in ink on or inside the book. These books are extremely popular at the book sale, and you'll want to keep the quality of this category high.

NEWER NONFICTION BOOKS

The quality and pricing of these books are similar to the category of Newer Fiction above. We are just separating the fiction from the nonfiction, which our customers seem to appreciate. These books are not separated into categories—simply Fiction and Nonfiction. Again, the books in this category are no more than six or seven years old and are in very nice condition. They often have the owner's name in them or some other minor markings, which is fine. Pencil the price lightly inside on the first page. Again, keep the quality high in this very popular category. The condition of the book is a major factor in determining where the book belongs. Experience and success at your sales will be your guide.

SETS

All book sets are priced individually, and the price and number of volumes in each set are noted inside the first volume of the set. We also list the year on encyclopedia and some other sets. For example, a 1999 30-volume set of the *Encyclopaedia Britannica* that you've decided you want to price at $75 should be penciled inside the first volume on right upper corner of first page as: —*1999 30 Vol/$75*. A general rule for pricing our sets is to start in your mind with $2 a volume, which is our base price for hardbacks. Then mark the set up

 TIP

If you sell all of your encyclopedia sets the first hour of the first day, the prices were probably too low.

(or occasionally down) depending on the year, the general condition, and the popularity of the set.

We have a volunteer who keeps a detailed record—a lined notebook page for each named set—with the date, the condition of the set, and the asking price. She has several binders: one for Time/Life and Reader's Digest sets (these are numerous), one for Children's sets, one for Encyclopedias, and a final binder for all other sets. During the sale she notes if the set sold at full price, half-price, or not at all. This information is an invaluable pricing tool. From this information, our sets chair also makes a list of sets that don't sell and then posts a Discontinued Sets listing in the sorting room. The sorters then know to discard these sets to the recycling bins (more about recycling later).

At our book sale last year we instituted a new process for displaying the sets for sale. We used a 3-by-5-inch index card and noted the name of the set, the year, the number of volumes, and the price. We then folded the bottom of this card so it would stand up as a tent card and placed this card on top of the set or sticking out of the first few pages. Shoppers could then walk by and tell at a glance what the set was selling for. Because the prices are so reasonable, many shoppers stopped to look who might otherwise have just dismissed the set. They could also quickly compare prices of the sets offered. When sets are purchased, the sellers keep these cards in a small box at the selling station, and these cards are given to the sets chair at the end of the sale for the records.

SPECIALLY PRICED BOOKS

These rare and collectible books make up about a third of our book sale profits. This was not always the case. In the past these books were about 10 percent of the total, but we have become very good at pulling the desirable collector books. This category is the difference between "good" and "great" book sales. Our sale draws dealers from all over the country. They know we have great books that are priced fairly. Although they may not find as many books on our base price tables that are worth thousands of dollars, they still appreciate the fair prices and quality of our offerings. These dealers leave a lot of money in our community for the library.

If a collectible book is in disrepair or missing illustrations, etc., we mark it down accordingly and state the condition in the front of the book. Review the Book Terms Glossary (appendix B) to become familiar with these book "points" terms. The books in the rare and collectible category have a minimum price of $3. Nancy Drew or a small Civil War book would start at $3, depending on the book. You can see the distinction between the specially priced books and other categories. The highest priced book for us (this was before our Internet sales began) was a signed Theodore Roosevelt book that we sold for $1,600! We're still looking for an original Lancaster County fraktur (hand-painted old Pennsylvania Dutch drawing) that would be worth thousands of dollars!

Potsdam sale pricing is similar to Lancaster's. They had established good relationship with a local used bookstore dealer to help in the identification and pricing of their collectible volumes.

Both Lancaster and Potsdam have another interesting pricing convention. We have a category called Light Romance, which is our gathering place for those skinny romance books (Harlequin, Silhouette, etc.). We get lots of these books and often had many of them left after our sales. A marketing strategy that has worked for us is to sell these books for $2.00 a bag—OUR bag. The bags are small vegetable bags that are donated from a local supermarket. Customers are happy—they can cram a dozen or so books in a bag, and we are selling books that we were throwing away at the end of our sale. Cheap price, but a good way to sell some slow-moving books. We've heard sale customers having a contest to see who could get the most in a bag. Even at this cheap price, some shoppers come with their list of books they are looking for—their favorite authors or titles.

Oro Valley has a volunteer who is a romance writer. She separates the romance novels into subcategories. For example, category romances (such as Silhouette and Harlequin), historical and regency romance, and romance divas (such as Danielle Steele, Nora Roberts, Diana Palmer) are some of the subcategories she has created. Attention to the romance section has greatly increased interest and sales for Oro Valley.

AN ALTERNATE STRATEGY FROM ORO VALLEY

Because we price every book, we don't use base-price and specially priced sections at our book sale. Due to space limitations and a smaller volunteer group, our pricers price and categorize each book, and then volunteers at the warehouse pack the books in the designated category boxes.

Our pricing guidelines are given to each pricer as they are trained. These prices are subject to book condition, of course. Pretty simply:

Hardcover fiction/mystery (full size in pristine condition) by date
- Current year: $7
- Previous year: $6
- 2 years old: $5
- 3 years old: $4
- 4 to 10 years old: $3
- Older books: $1–$2 ($1 lower for book club, library discards, not pristine condition, etc.)

Trade paperback by original list price
- $12.95 and under: $3
- Over $12.95: $4

Mass-market paperback by age
- 5 years old or newer: $2
- 6 years old or older: $1 or 50 cents (condition plays a big part in this pricing)

"Tall" mass market by original list price
- $9.99: $3

Our nonfiction categories follow this guideline with the added concerns: Is this book still relevant (or is it just an old high school textbook)? Is this subject matter interesting to our customers (or is a listing of prices for bed-and-breakfasts from 1980 outdated)?

A lot of our nonfiction does get quick research online to help with pricing (the going price on Amazon, for instance). We place all books in the same category together in our sale, regardless of publishing date, so people looking for any sports book (brand-new or an "oldie") will find it under the sports category.

Audiobooks are priced at one-third of list price. We sell music CDs for $3 per disc and DVDs for $4 per disc.

We have purchased a machine for our library that removes scratches and cleans CDs and DVDs. We use this to clean the merchandise that we put out for sale. We are considering whether to discontinue sales of VHS and cassettes. Too many are left after the sale.

....

Set prices to sell. There's no point in doing all this work if you're not going to sell merchandise at a fair price. This is a learning process. Most old textbooks do not sell, even at fifty cents. A John Steinbeck first edition, on the other hand, sells for a lot—and quickly! These are all things that you will learn along the way. Experience is the best teacher. One important lesson we've learned through the years is that it's all about having the right books at the right time. What sells one year may not be a big seller the next year. Or that person who loved and bought all your science books moved away. It's a funny thing, this marketing game. We don't claim to be experts, but we have become experienced at knowing our customers and our product. You will too.

7

Venue and Promotion

Sale Scheduling and Publicity

 TIP

Consistency in date as well as site will help your sale stay in customers' minds and on their calendars.

It's time to schedule your sale and start letting people know about it. Choosing the right place for your big event will set the stage for success; publicity is crucial to ensure that you draw the audience to fill your venue.

First carefully select your site, reviewing the advantages and disadvantages of each location. Think of your local library first, and if it's not suitable, make a listing of all other potential locations in your area. Use your volunteer resources and the library board of trustees to find a possible benefactor to underwrite facility costs.

Discuss the timing and duration of your sale. When will you be ready to launch your sale? Is the timing good with regard to other community events or holidays, or should you postpone the sale to a more opportune date? How many hours of volunteer time will you be able to secure?

SALE CONSIDERATIONS— WHERE/WHEN/HOW OFTEN

You will want to give careful consideration to finding a suitable site for your book sale. There are lots of options to explore before you make a final decision. Keeping the same site from year to year, when possible, helps with continuity and gives a permanent feeling to your sale. Timing of the sale is also important and can increase your success significantly.

Sale Site Considerations

An ideal book sale site will have lots of parking, a great location, plenty of room inside to display your books to their best advantage, and good lighting—and will be free. Tall order! Get as many of those qualities as you can for the site you select. Price of the facility is a major consideration. Many sales have a space donated, and some book sales pay only a reduced price to cover the facility expenses. Negotiate the best deal you can. A library trustee may have some insights or influence into community sites that would be suitable. Of course, your local library is a wonderful place for a sale, providing there is sufficient room.

When Should You Have Your Sale? Should You Have an Annual Sale or Several Mini-Sales?

As you've probably already surmised, a book sale requires a lot of work—and we haven't yet talked about setup, running a sale, or cleanup! So, be careful about planning too many events in a year. An annual sale is usually enough for a group of inexperienced volunteers to handle. An occasional small sale at a town fair or community day event is also not too difficult to plan. You will already have a supply of sorted books and can quickly set up a few folding tables to sell a small quantity of books.

For your big annual event, pick the date and times carefully. You will want to get a community calendar to see what types of events you will be competing with, or events that may complement your sale. Of course, sometimes the facility where you're holding your event may have limited dates available. Once you've settled on a site, book it a year in advance if possible.

Details from Our Sales

Lancaster

Our big annual sale is held at a local college sports center in the spring of each year. We book the facility in advance, and we take every opportunity throughout the year to keep those dates in the public eye. Bookmarks at the library, publicity about our sale efforts during the year, and our book donation drop-offs once a month are all opportunities to remind the public of our big event.

For forty years our book sales were held in the library. We loved having the sale there. Many people came to the library to attend the sale and got their first library card while there. Also, the library staff, while putting up with the disruption, felt very much a part of the sale. The staff personally saw how much work the volunteers did in support of the library. However, renovations to the library, including installation of computers, limited the available open space. Our sale was also growing each year, so we had to look for another facility. The college sports center was a great solution to our site problem. The facility has room for the book sale to expand, and it should accommodate our sale for years to come.

Our big spring sale is held Monday through Wednesday. The sale hours are 7 a.m. to 9 p.m. on Monday. (The early-bird opening not only offers working people a chance to shop for books before work, but many out-of-town people are literally camped out in the parking lot overnight and eager to start buying books.) Our hours on Tuesday are 9 a.m. to 9 p.m., and on Wednesday, 9 a.m. to 6 p.m.. We have to be out of the facility Wednesday night, as college activities start the next day. The 6 p.m. closing gives us several hours to clean up after the sale, and by 9 p.m. the facility is transformed back to a sports center.

Potsdam

Potsdam's first big annual sale was held at a hockey rink donated by a local university. They used about two-thirds of the rink, and they held book signings and other activities in conjunction with the sale, which was a huge success. The sale was held in May to coincide with university graduations and lots of out-of-town parents visiting the town. The sale opened on Friday from noon to 8 p.m. Saturday hours were 9 a.m. to 6 p.m., and Sunday hours were 9 a.m. to 5 p.m. The facility was great—and free!—with lots of parking.

Oro Valley

In Oro Valley we do have a spring and a fall sale, both in the library. We use a large meeting room plus other parts of the library, and we normally have over 20,000 books for sale. Our sales are four-day events—Wednesday through Saturday. The sale hours coincide with the library's operating hours: Wednesday, Friday, and Saturday from 9 a.m. to 5 p.m. and Thursday from 11 a.m. to 8 p.m.

PUBLICITY FOR YOUR BOOK SALE

"If you have a book sale, they will come" is true, but only if "they" know about it! Library book sales are increasing in popularity in direct proportion to the skyrocketing prices of new books, and also in relation to tough economic conditions. You have a most desirable product in your used books, and you just need to let people know about your sale. Listed below are some basic publicity ideas. We have included some creative ones that have worked well for our book sales.

Prepare a Fact Sheet about Your Book Sale

Before you decide on how and where you will advertise your book sale, get the information about your sale down on paper. List location, dates, times, how many books, and what categories will be offered for sale—all the pertinent information. Be sure to have several people review and proofread your fact sheet. There is so much chance for error in spelling, dates, times, and the like. You also need to make sure that the information is correct and that your project is represented in every aspect—publications, sound clips, etc.—with a unified voice.

WHERE TO PUBLICIZE THE BOOK SALE

There are so many places and opportunities to spread the word about your sale, most of them free!

Local Radio and TV Stations, Newspapers and Other Local Publications

A book sale that supports your community library is always good news locally. It is important to make local contacts with these publicity outlets and to give them written information about your sale. See the book sale press release (fig. 7.1), which was developed directly from the sale fact sheet. Compile a listing of the places where you will send this press release.

Oro Valley was invited to be interviewed on *The Morning Blend* on local Tucson TV. We were able to not only talk about the upcoming spring books sale, but also about our two bookshops and our online offerings. A few days later we were on a local call-in radio show. All of this was wonderful publicity going out to different audiences.

One important comment about newspapers: push for placement on the front or back page of the newspaper, or at least the front page of the local section. If you don't discuss the placement of your article, it might be buried in the style section on the inside column near the bottom. Speak up—this is important community stuff! Nurturing relationships with a few reporters from the local TV station or newspaper helps, too.

In addition to sending the generic press release, providing an exclusive story or suggesting creative angles will help you get better placement for your book sale information. You can get much free publicity if you develop a special angle or creative idea that the newspaper or television station can expand into a great lengthy article or interview. Here are a few of the ideas we peddled to the media that turned into wonderful, free publicity for us.

High-Interest Titles

Several newspaper articles featured rare book finds that Lancaster offers at their sale. These special finds included books autographed by Richard Nixon, Martin Luther King Jr., and W. C. Fields, as well as Mark Twain first editions and books illustrated by N. C. Wyeth and Maxfield Parrish. As you sort books throughout the year, keep a list of interesting books or collections of books that could be used for publicity purposes. Last year we had a tremendous amount of beautiful large-print books—a very popular category—and we emphasized that in some of our publicity. Lancaster also had a feature article

FROM: Jane Doe, Publicity Chair
SUBJECT: Lancaster Public Library Book Sale
DATE: April 15, 2000

FOR IMMEDIATE RELEASE
The Lancaster Public Library 46th Annual Book Sale will be held May 3–5, 2000, at Franklin & Marshall College Sports Center. This ever-popular community event will have over 150,000 books for sale. The books are sorted into 39 categories, with something for everyone. Over half of the books offered will be priced at $2 a volume. Other more current, gift-quality, and rare books will be priced at $3 or more.

The sale begins on Monday, May 3, 2000, with an early-bird opening at 7 a.m. The sale closes Monday night at 9 p.m., and on Tuesday, May 4, from 9 a.m. to 6 p.m.

All book sale proceeds benefit the Lancaster Public Library. This sale is a great way to get some wonderful inexpensive books while supporting the Lancaster Library.

Figure 7.1 `WEB`
Sample book sale press release. Press releases should be printed on official Friends or Library letterhead.

written one year on the used-bookstore owner who donated his time and expertise to help the sale get fair prices for their collectible books.

Hidden Treasure

One year the local TV station did a five-minute news spot directly from Lancaster's sale on the "treasures" found in donated books. Many of the unusual items were brought to the sale, and the reporter did a great job talking about the marriage licenses, diaries, photos, lottery tickets, money, and other crazy items that people use to mark their place in a book. That TV exposure brought in lots of customers during the next two days of the book sale.

Poster Contest

Potsdam got some great publicity by sponsoring a book sale poster contest in the local schools. The winners were awarded prizes donated by local merchants, and the local papers sent a reporter to interview and photograph the winners. This was great publicity for their first annual spring book sale. Lancaster jumped on this idea and ran a successful poster contest, too. Winners and winning posters were featured at the book sale.

Volunteer Spotlight

Several years ago a local Lancaster boy earned his Eagle Scout badge by helping with a book sale project. At that time we used sawhorses and plywood as tables. The sawhorses were too short, and he designed and produced wooden pieces to raise the height. At his direction, he and his fellow troop members made and placed these tops on 320 sawhorses. He was interviewed, and his troop, family, and the book sale got some great publicity. In an earlier year, the local vocational school made sorting tables for Lancaster. The cameras snapped, and the book sale got some great publicity in the Lancaster *Sunday News* right before the sale.

The Internet

A wonderful place to advertise your book sale or bookstore in a big way is the Internet. The website www .booksalefinder.com is a site visited regularly by professionals in the used-book business, as well as others browsing for book sales. Have a volunteer list your information on this free website, give an e-mail address for inquiries, and answer e-mail questions. This site is also a good resource for your book sale—you can visit and research book sales near you or just browse

TIP

Tent-card posters reproduced on sturdy cardstock work well on restaurant tables, and bookmarks take up little room on a counter.

through the listings to see what other sales are doing, including their book pricing ranges. People at our book sales—many of them vacationers—tell us they found out about our sale on the Internet. The wonders of technology are making the world a smaller and most interesting place.

Your Own Mailing Lists

Develop your own mail and e-mail lists for sending book sale information and brochures with the pertinent book sale information from your fact sheet. For an easy mailing, use a trifolded piece of 8.5-by-11-inch paper, stapled or taped shut, with a label on the outside. To develop your list, start with your local bookstore owners, check on the Internet for stores in surrounding counties, and have a mailing/e-mail request list sign-up sheet at your sales. A few stamps can pay big dividends. Your list will grow quickly and will need to be kept current. Developing a good e-mail list will save postage and time, and busy people may be more likely to read an e-mail than pay attention to a flyer received in the mail.

Bookmarks and Posters

A great way to reach people who miss your newspaper articles is extensive distribution of posters on community bulletin boards, in the library, or in any stores that will allow you to put them up. Be gracious to the storeowner, but lay it on thick about "all proceeds benefit the local library." You will find, as we have, that a great community spirit surrounds the library and its importance to your town. Be sure to remove posters after the sale, so your next sale posters will be welcome. Offering posters in several sizes, even some small ones, will give you more options for placement, as some establishments will not put up large posters. We also make lots of small poster handouts—4.25 by 5.5 inches, which equals two to a sheet of 8.5-by-11-inch

paper. Some stores and restaurants allow us to leave a small stack of these on their counter, and customers can take a copy with them. These are very popular, and the customer has a personal copy as a reminder (see fig. 7.2). Bookmarks work well, too, and the circulation desk at the library can give these out to customers as they check out books.

Paid Advertising

Sometimes a targeted paid advertisement reaps benefits. Each year Lancaster places a small, inexpensive ad in a local public television magazine that reaches across five surrounding counties. This magazine has a large circulation, and many book lovers at our sales tell us they saw our ad in this publication.

We also have occasionally bought a paid radio ad from a popular station in an adjacent county that reaches into several counties near Philadelphia. We talked to some customers who came to the sale because of this ad. It is very hard to gauge the effectiveness of these ads; we rely on customer feedback.

Oro Valley buys ads in the local section of their newspaper. They also pay for a thank-you ad when the sale is over addressed to all those who donated time, books, or services to help make their sale a success.

Publicity is critical to the success of your sale. Prepare the fact sheet carefully and get your information out in plenty of time for the media to meet deadlines. Using interesting angles will help you get stories written about your sale, rather than just a listing of the date and time.

Be sure to cover a large geographic area. People who love books will drive way out of their way to shop at a book sale. Get your sale listed on the Internet. The whole country and beyond will see your information. The Potsdam sale had customers from Canada and Vermont who saw the sale listed online. Lancaster draws customers from around the country. Oro Valley has had repeat shoppers from California and other neighboring states.

Use your volunteers to distribute posters, bookmarks, and tent cards. Keep a listing of where volunteers are placing these items so that you get good coverage. Ask your library to put posters and place bookmarks in surrounding libraries.

Figure 7.2
Sample promotional poster. Create promotional posters in multiple sizes, including an easy to pick up
4.25-by-5.5-inch version.

8

Showtime

Book Sale Days, Setup through Cleanup

 TIP

Have key workers on the sale floor wear carpenter's aprons (perhaps with your Friends logo printed on them) that have pockets to carry paper, pencil, small battery-operated calculators, and the like.

The books are sorted, the volunteers are ready, the place and time have been selected, the publicity is out, and customers are saving their money to buy your books. All you have to do is throw the books on some tables, right? Oh, if only that were true! There is still much to consider.

PRESALE ACTIVITIES

Draw a Sale Layout Plan

The easiest way we have found to make a layout for a book sale is to use graph paper. This will ensure that the dimensions will be fairly accurate. You don't need much artistic ability to count off squares where one graph paper block equals one foot, or something similar. Measure your facility carefully, and note entrances, doorways, rest rooms, barriers, etc. on your drawing. After we had a final graph paper drawing, we re-created it using Excel (fig. 8.1). A computer-generated layout is not necessary for setup; your pencil drawing is sufficient. But if you plan to hand out floor plan maps at your sale, an Excel version will be easier to reproduce and easier for customers to read.

To prepare the drawing you will need graph paper, a pencil, a ruler, and a *big* eraser. You will also need your list of the number of sorted boxes by category, the dimensions of the sale facility, and a lot of patience. On your graph paper, clearly note the number of tables you will need for each category and the distance between tables. Because Lancaster has a large facility, we can make 6-foot-wide aisles. These aisles accommodate wheelchairs and baby strollers, and all shoppers enjoy the space. Some local fire codes may mandate aisle widths, so check with your municipality. In Lancaster we have to submit a drawing to the city fire company, and they also come out to check the facility for safety features. Mark the location of your cashier stations on the layout. Your facility will dictate the most strategic placement for your checkout tables to control shoppers as they exit.

The Lancaster sale splits the sale area of the facility, using part for the unmarked base price books and the rest for the individually priced books. A barrier of stanchions with helium-filled balloons placed along the tapes from the stanchions works for us. This high-flying separation helps to distinctly mark the higher-priced books section, and also serves as a frame of reference when directing customers to a specific category during the sale. Both Lancaster and Oro Valley now use the tally table system (described in detail in chapter 9), where customers take their purchases to a tally table to be counted and bagged before proceeding to a cashier for payment of their purchases.

Order All Setup Materials

If you are renting folding tables, arrange to have them delivered at the correct time and place. Follow up any telephone contact with a confirmation letter so there is no misunderstanding about your requirements.

Make Final Contact with the Facility Manager

Request that a knowledgeable facility contact person be on-site during the sale and get necessary telephone numbers for facility personnel. You will also need to know the mechanics of the facility—who opens and locks up and at what time, who should be called if there is

TIP

Consider instituting an express line, with a sign stating *About 12 Items*.

a plumbing or other facility problem, where the light switches, fuse boxes, and other necessary building services are, and whether there is a locked room that can be used as a "command post" for the sale. At the Lancaster sale there is a locked room where money is counted and receipts and other sale supplies are kept. There is also a secure storage room where volunteers can put their personal belongings during the sale.

Make Arrangements to Transport Books

If your sale is at a site other than your sorting facility, make the necessary arrangements to have books transported to your sale site. Again, a phone call followed up by a confirmation letter is the best way to avoid any misunderstanding as to the sequence of events. This is important—no books, no sale! Lancaster is lucky enough to have a local trucking company donate a driver and five tractor-trailers to transport their mountain of books. In Oro Valley a local moving company donates trucks, labor, and time to help move books from the sorting site to the library for their book sale.

Besides all the wonderful volunteers who help Lancaster, work-release inmates help with the heavy lifting and moving of the books, and also are there for setup and cleanup assistance. These work-release helpers have been a blessing, and the community involvement these helpers see and participate in is quite an experience for all. The helpers are carefully selected at the correction facility (many of them hold full-time jobs in the community); usually those chosen are in jail for nonsupport or driving under the influence. The work-release people really enjoy coming to help us. They and the book sale volunteers learn a lot about each other and themselves. For over twenty years, this arrangement has been a mutually rewarding endeavor. The workers may also take three books each back to the prison (the limit is set by the prison). Contact your sheriff's office or correctional facility to see if there is an opportunity in your community for this type of help.

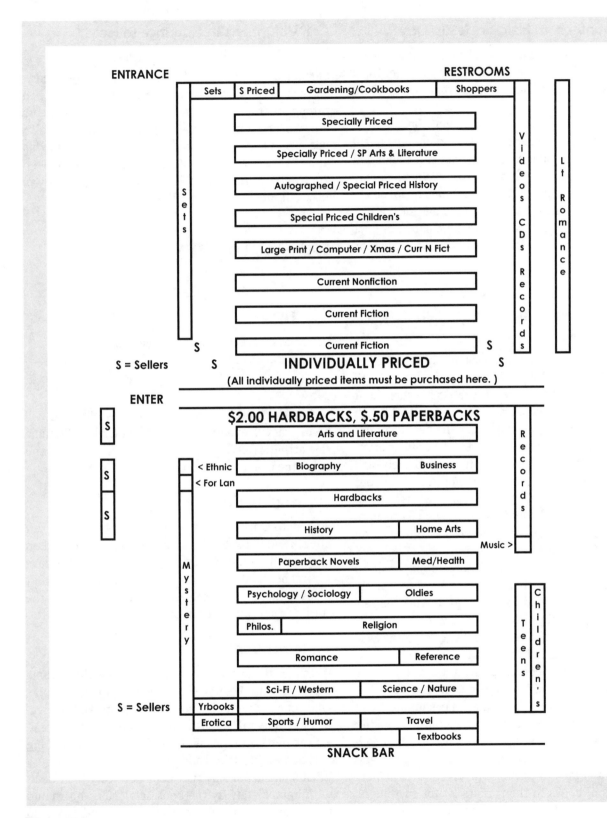

Figure 8.1

Sample book sale floor plan.

Call Volunteers to Help on Setup Day

You will need many volunteers to help with the unloading and unpacking of your books for the sale. Have several people make calls to get a commitment from helpers.

Lancaster and Oro Valley both provide lunch for the core setup people. If your setup will require only a few hours' work, you might want to provide just drinks and an easy snack like pretzels or popcorn. Volunteers may not bring children under 12 years old to help, for safety reasons as well as to preserve some order for the day. Parents who need to supervise young children are not the most productive workers and can cause disruptions to a busy setup process.

Call Volunteers in Advance to Help during the Book Sale

Get your volunteers lined up for selling shifts and other help you will need during the sale. Make sure that all your workstations are covered. Lancaster has three-hour shifts and puts two volunteers at each station. When calling these volunteers, emphasize the need to honor their shift commitments. If unforeseen conflicts arise, ask that the affected volunteers try to find their own substitutes to cover the time slot. You will have your hands full with other sale activities, and juggling schedules and making last-minute calls for workers need to be kept to a minimum. Lancaster does assign a person to handle these last-minute changes.

Besides tally and cashier volunteers (explanation of these functions in chapter 9), we have five or six *floor workers*—seasoned volunteers who work the sale straightening books, answering questions, directing people to specific categories, and anything else needed in the midst of the crowd. These floor workers should be knowledgeable, energetic, and friendly people. You will find that the neater you keep the books on the tables, the neater the shoppers will keep them. Also, having the books visible and looking orderly sells more books. Lancaster also has two daytime work-release volunteers during the sale. A volunteer is assigned to direct their tasks. These helpers take carts of books to the parking lot for customers, move tables if required, put up additional signs, and perform any other miscellaneous tasks that may need attention.

Call Volunteers in Advance to Help on Cleanup Day

Cleanup after the book sale requires a lot of volunteers, and it most certainly will include people who have helped throughout the sale. Again, the work-release volunteers are critical to our huge cleanup efforts. Lancaster also has a Boy Scout troop and leaders who help in this effort every year, and Oro Valley has teens from the Teen Zone in the library who help with setup and teardown. Make all these contacts well in advance of your sale.

SALE ACTIVITIES

 TIP

Do *not* let shoppers in to browse before the sale. (Some *will* ask to do this.)

During the book sale, any or all of the following will occur. You will eventually build your own list of unique sale activities. To start, though, go with the flow, and enjoy the event that will take on a life of its own.

Opening the Sale

Be sure to start the sale on time—not before and not after the advertised time. In Lancaster, several hundred people will be in line waiting for the opening. We have several book sale volunteers who hand out sale layout maps to those waiting. Open the doors promptly at the starting time, and get out of the way!

Customer Contacts

Watch for those very few book shoppers who become rude or unruly. We have had only occasional shoppers who got a little out of hand over the years, and we gently but firmly talked with them. Sometimes book dealers can get a little pushy—book sale shopping is a big part of their livelihood and profits—but these are very isolated incidents. Any rude behavior needs to be dealt with immediately by the book sale chair. You should not be concerned about this issue, just aware. We do welcome booksellers with open arms—they leave a lot of money in our towns for our libraries!

CUSTOMER REQUESTS

During a recent book sale, Pat received an urgent cell phone call from a customer en route from Delaware to the Pennsylvania sale. He had a favor to ask of her: "Would you please run over to the History and Biography sections and tell the shoppers there that there's an emergency and they must evacuate. I will be there shortly to purchase my books in that area. I am wearing plaid shirt, tan slacks, and suspenders." Pat suggested he put a rose in his teeth so she would recognize him. He did indeed arrive, seek her out, and purchase a lot of books!

PREVIEW SALES

Many book sales have a preview the night before the sale starts, and there is an admission charge—often ranging from $5 to $25. Years ago Lancaster held a preview night during the 40th book sale anniversary celebration. A wine and cheese party was held for the community, and the book sale was open, but the number of collectible books that could be purchased was limited to ten books. Some dealers did come and paid the $25 admission fee. Most customers, however, were library patrons. Lancaster has not held another preview night and has no plans to hold a preview in the foreseeable future.

A few years ago, Oro Valley held a preview night prior to the opening of the book sale. In order to enter the book sale, customers who were not members of the Friends of the Library had to pay the membership fee at the door. This preview night was not only poorly attended, but because our sale is held in the library, library patrons were upset with this idea. Oro Valley has not held another preview night. Many libraries do hold successful sale previews. Decide what will work best for your book sale.

Keep your ears open for comments, both good and bad, as you proceed through the sale. Every few years we put out a suggestion box. We do take these suggestions seriously, and many of our improvements have been a direct result of these suggestions from our shoppers. Some of the comments are great, some are helpful, some are legitimate complaints, and some of the suggestions are downright funny! One shopper in Oro Valley, a retired librarian, had dared to hope the books could be arranged in Dewey Decimal System order. Another suggestion was to have only two categories—Fiction and Nonfiction. That certainly would simplify things for us!

There has been a lot of discussion and controversy about customers using their own electronic scanners at the sale. We feel that unless the person using the scanner is being unruly or disruptive, there is no reason to ban these devices. In fact, many of these customers are buying large quantities of books. Some are book scouts, buying books to sell to bookstores or larger dealers, and some are selling online themselves. Just be watchful that these shoppers do not create piles of books that they then abandon for you to deal with.

The sale is a great opportunity to sign up new volunteers. These shoppers are book lovers. Always have volunteer forms or pencil and paper on hand to get names and phone numbers of these potential volunteers. Many of our current volunteers started out as customers at book sales, including us!

Watch for erupting problems and diffuse them quickly. Improperly marked merchandise, a blocked car in the parking lot, a lost child—all these are issues that any retailer deals with regularly.

Book Prices

Do not negotiate prices. All questions regarding pricing should be referred to the book sale chair or designate. Lancaster's books sales run for three days, and days one and two are full price—no exceptions. At the opening of the third day all books are half-price. Advance publicity clearly states this third day as half-price day, so you will get customers coming back for bargains. On this final day of the sale, watch for opportunities to sell books—someone who's been looking at a twenty-volume encyclopedia set and is wavering in the decision just might take this bulky set off your hands for a few dollars under the asking price. Just remember that it is the book sale chair or designate who must make this decision.

Details from Our Sales

Lancaster

Lancaster used to sell books for $5 per brown grocery bag for the last three hours of the sale. We have discontinued this practice and instead leave books at half price for all the final day. The bag sale became too unwieldy for the large amount of customers we have. We had to make all shoppers check out the books they had already selected, clear the floor, and *then* begin the bag sale. Some shoppers, knowing the bag sale was eminent, would stash books under the table, hoping to recoup them at the bag sale price. Other shoppers resented having to check out their books and clear the floor. We had fun with it for a lot of years, announcing the activity and making a sort of circus atmosphere. Although a few customers were unhappy about the demise of the bag sale (mostly dealers!), our volunteers are delighted that we've discontinued this practice. Because our book broker sells many of our leftover books online for us, we don't feel as much pressure to wring every dollar out of these books at the sale itself.

Oro Valley

Conversely, at Oro Valley, after two days of full-price books and a day and a half of half-price books, the last four hours of their sale has books selling for $5 per brown grocery bag, which Oro Valley supplies. As the bag sale time nears, customers in line get very excited about helping open and double the bags to be used. The waiting generates a party atmosphere, and when our chair finishes the countdown—"10 . . . 9 . . . 8 . . ."— the line rushes in and the room fills nearly to bursting with happy shoppers.

By the last day of the sale, you are looking to unload books. You may want to have a few seasoned volunteers pull a couple of boxes of selected nice books that

may be marketable in your bookstore, but keep this to a minimum. Some book sales make the mistake of keeping too many unsold books and bringing them out for the next sale. Offering the same leftovers too many times will give your sale a bad reputation. There's usually a reason why those books didn't sell! If you follow our advice about receiving book donations, you should have no trouble having a steady supply of new donations to offer at your future sales.

Marketing Opportunities during the Sale

Think of creative ways to sell slow-moving books. For example, if the travel books are not getting much customer attention, try moving them to an area where there's more traffic. As your sale proceeds, you will have spaces opening up to allow you to do this shifting. Add signs at the Children's tables that direct people to the specially priced books—"Check out the special price Children's section for beautiful books priced $2 and up."

Invite and entice television and newspaper reporters and photographers to come when your sale is in progress. Lancaster has been very fortunate to get on the local television news reports, and many people come out to the book sales because of this local coverage. Last year a TV reporter and cameraman were there before our opening to interview people in line—there were about five hundred people gathered before our 7 a.m. opening. The cameraman then caught the images of people running into the sale when the doors opened. That spot was shown live on the morning and noon broadcasts.

Try to set up a time when your book sale chair can be available to meet with reporters. The reporters will likely interview some of your customers also. The pictures the newspaper photographers have gotten at Lancaster are priceless—a teenager totally engrossed in a book and oblivious to the crowds of shoppers, a group of young children sprawled on the floor showing their favorite books to each other, a man surrounded by boxes of classical records he was purchasing. This man comes to the book sale every year from Cleveland, where he plays in the Cleveland Symphony. In the reporter's interview, the gentleman said that he had to stop buying because that's all that would fit in his van. All these images and interviews are great publicity. Lancaster sale also showed up on many YouTube videos, some as feeds from reporters and some from local volunteers (see, for example, http://youtu.be./fBP2Y68WVTM).

TIP

If you have a loudspeaker system or a battery-powered bullhorn, try running a "blue-light special" à la Kmart for a specific book category that needs some special attention or excitement.

Taking Care of Your Volunteers

Make sure your volunteers are made to feel that they are an integral and important part of your book sale team. Make name tags for them so they can get to know one another and are also easily identifiable as being part of the book sale team. We also have official-looking lanyards with name tags for key committee people to wear at the sale.

See that the volunteers know exactly what is required of them. Have typed instructions at each checkout station so that these volunteers feel very comfortable with their duties. If you have a "command post" room, post the latest book sale totals there so everyone can see how much money is being made. Give volunteers a safe, secure place to leave their personal belongings. If sale activity has a lull, have someone relieve the volunteer at their station for fifteen or twenty minutes so they can take a little break and perhaps browse a little, too. Place a number on the tally and cashier stations so volunteers can get their bearings quickly and know where they are assigned to work.

CLOSING THE SALE EACH DAY

It is a good idea to have a few volunteers available who agree to stay a little past your stated closing time. Make sure someone is in charge of announcing the impending closing time and directing shoppers to the checkout stations. If you have twenty-five or so shoppers still buying books, you could consider staying open an extra fifteen minutes, depending on your facility's rules. However, book lovers are a unique breed. Some will stay until you literally throw them out! You will have to deal with this each day of your sale. Do not put too much extra burden on your volunteers just to accommodate a few shoppers.

Postsale Activities

The book sale team has done all the hard work preparing for and then running the book sale. It's the last day of the sale, and you and your volunteers are dog tired. Guess what? Now you have to clean up! This is the tough part, and it will take all your skills to keep your volunteers motivated. What we have found, however, is that the adrenaline continues to flow. A little advance planning will make the cleanup go smoothly.

Consolidation

As your book sale winds down in its last few hours, a few handpicked volunteers can consolidate tables where possible, pick out the *few* boxes you may want to keep for your next sale, and generally get ready for your cleanup effort. In Lancaster several dozen empty tables are dismantled before the sale is officially over. Just be sure to let the shopping continue as you do this low-key consolidation. Every book sold is one less to clean up!

Leftover Books

Now there is a problem that has no easy answer. You *will* have leftover books—in Lancaster there are traditionally about 10 percent of the books remaining at the end of the sale. Since Lancaster takes about 250,000 books to this huge sale, there will be about 25,000 unsold books at the end of the sale. There are only so many copies of *The Thorn Birds* and *The Da Vinci Code* you can sell. And we won't even mention the ubiquitous Danielle Steel novels.

There are some options here. Some sales actually keep many of their leftover books and put them out for future sales. This practice is not recommended, and avid book shoppers steer clear of sales that continually have the same unsellable books at their sales.

For several years the nicer Lancaster leftovers were trucked 420 miles north to Potsdam. Potsdam Friends had just started their sale and did not have a lot of donated books, and they made thousands of dollars from these Lancaster books. Taking the books to Potsdam was a good business decision. The interest generated in Potsdam and the new donations they received because of their successful sale was most appreciated.

TIP

Consider asking for leftovers from another book sale to help jump-start your sale. For the past few years, Oro Valley has received the still-saleable remains of the Tucson Brandeis University sale to supplement their own book sale.

Details from Our Sales

Lancaster

Lancaster had a book wholesaler in the past who also took away the mountain of unsold books from our big spring sale (about 55 to 60 gaylords full!) They paid us a small amount for these leftover books and would then sell some of them online and recycle the unsellable items. We did not share in the profits from these online sales.

We now use a different book broker, Giggil (an acronym for "*Green is good, good is less*," emphasizing their recycling focus). The contract calls for Giggil (www.giggil.com) to bring gaylords to our sale facility and wooden pallets to set them on. The gaylords are placed strategically around the book sale floor, and the volunteers place leftover sale books in them. Our books are trucked to the Giggil processing facility, where the unsellable books are removed for recycling. Giggil then transports the sellable items to Amazon. These books are identified as belonging to Lancaster, and when any of them sell on Amazon, we share in the profits, after a processing fee is deducted by the broker. This results in more profits for Lancaster, as many good books are unsold at the end of our sale. Giggil

 TIP

A *gaylord* is a reusable large cardboard container often about 4-feet high and 4-feet wide that holds about a thousand pounds of books. These corrugated containers were originally manufactured by the Gaylord Container Company, and this terminology is used by many of the book haulers.

also takes away our sorting discards throughout the year. The discards are placed in gaylords after each of our work sessions. When ten or so gaylords are filled, the broker brings a truck and takes the full gaylords away, leaving empty ones to start the process again.

Although we are new with Giggil, the results so far have been very promising, with some monthly checks coming in for sales they made on our behalf through Amazon. Detailed reports of those sales are being developed so we can see which books sold and at what price, as well as the processing fees deducted by Giggil.

There are other book brokers serving libraries, such as Better World Books (betterworldbooks.com). Do your own research to see what book wholesalers are available in your area and what type of arrangement you can negotiate. Leftover books are a valuable commodity, so be assertive in your negotiations to strike the best deal for your organization. You have to find what works best for you. In any case, don't be discouraged if you can't find a buyer for your smaller sale books. Other libraries would probably be willing and eager to incorporate your books into their next sale. Oro Valley is pleased to get the Brandeis books, and they now help out another library as well. If no other library in your region is interested, try local charitable organizations.

Oro Valley

For several years, Oro Valley was able to find book dealers eager to buy their sale leftovers. While they still attempt to locate buyers for these books, they do have to be out of their area in the library as soon as possible so the library can get back to business. They do not have storage space to allow them time to wait for a buyer. In that light, they recently donated books to another local library sale, and their current sale leftovers were given to a well-respected local nonprofit charity, World Care Tucson. In the future they hope to resume selling their end-of-sale books.

Packing Up after the Book Sale

The Oro Valley sale has the "luxury" of having two days to unwind their sale held in a large meeting room and other areas of the library. To accomplish this, they have to get volunteers to work on a Sunday (not an easy task). Lancaster must be out of the sports facility three or four hours after the sale closes, so an efficient and speedy cleanup plan is critical. The book broker who picks up Lancaster's unsold books brings gaylords, and volunteers literally dump the books in these bins. Carts go whizzing by loaded with books, and in no time at all the books are packed and loaded onto the broker's tractor trailers. Tables are quickly dismantled, and the category signs are carefully taken down and packed to be ready for the next sale.

Your goal is to leave the facility exactly the way you found it. Dispose of any trash accumulated during the sale. Your facility may let you use their Dumpster; otherwise you need to pack up your trash and take it with you. Be a good tenant so you will be welcomed back.

Sale Proceeds Total

While the rest of the volunteers are involved in the cleanup, the selling chair and his team make the final count of the book sale proceeds. They keep up with the money count except for the last few hours, so it does not take too long to come up with the preliminary total. It is a great idea to let the book sale chair announce the total gross proceeds to the cleanup crew. A call reporting the final total to the local newspaper is also a good idea.

Wrap-up Meeting

Within several weeks after the book sale, when you have all had a chance to catch your breath, plan a wrap-up meeting. Lancaster uses the occasion to celebrate their success, with a dinner attended by the book sale committee members and invited guests. The library board president, the executive director of the library, and several library staff members who work directly on book sale issues are invited guests, but committee members pay for their own meals. At this festive dinner, several people give short congratulatory messages and thank-yous. Prior to the dinner, the book sale committee meets to talk about the sale. Committee chairs give reports, including the final sales figures for the book sale. This meeting gives the committee the opportunity to talk about what went right and what can be improved upon. The sale is still very fresh in everyone's mind, and now is the time to discuss these ideas.

Thank-you Notes

There are many people who should be thanked in writing for their participation in the book sale. Lancaster's selling chairs send a photocopied note with a few added personal comments to each volunteer who worked a selling shift at the sale. The total proceeds from the sale are noted in the letter, and the letter thanks each of them for helping the library. For community donations of goods or services to the book sale, a thank-you letter should be sent on Friends letterhead. Lancaster sends notes to the local trucking firm that donates trucks and a driver, and to many others who share in the book sale success. A letter to the editor is sent to the local newspaper thanking community sponsors, volunteers, and especially the community who donated the books and then shopped at the sale. Oro Valley also sends letters to those who have offered their services and buys a newspaper advertisement to thank their volunteers, community partners, and everyone who supported the sale.

The book sale event takes a lot of coordination and planning. Many activities need to be completed long before the event. With so many aspects to coordinate, it helps to delegate some very specific tasks to selected volunteers. The book sale chair should, however, check in with these volunteers periodically to make sure that all the pieces are in place. Not everything will go according to plan, particularly when your sale is new and your group is in the learning phase. Take the most care with the big items, and if a few small ones don't come together perfectly, then you have something to improve for the next year.

If you hold a book sale they will come, and you can be assured of customers coming the first time. Making them want to return for your next sale takes a little more planning. Document your processes along the way and learn from your missteps. Names and telephone numbers of important contacts and volunteers, samples of your layout, ideas for future sales—are all critical to collect and record.

Keep the book sale event under control, but make it fun, too. A book sale is a lot of work, but so, so rewarding. Your library and community will reap the benefits of your team's hard work.

9

Box Office Receipts

Keeping Account of Your Sales Income

We have shown you how you can make money for your library. The next step is to safeguard the money you collect and account for it properly. This is a critical part of fundraising, and those who have not been diligent and honest with monies raised in the name of nonprofit organizations have been ostracized and, in some cases, jailed. We will tell you how to set up your tally and cashier tables at the sale, how to account for your sales dollars, and what other precautions to take to protect the funds you raise.

TALLY/CASHIER TABLES AT YOUR BOOK SALE

You will need tally tables and cashier stations at your sale exit. How many you need will depend on the size and characteristics of your facility as well as the number of volunteers available. The tally tables (include chairs, too!) are where your volunteers will count and bag or box each customer's books, using a book sale tally form (fig. 9.1).

 TIP

Lancaster followed Oro Valley's successful lead in using credit-card machines. Sharing ideas with other book sales is invaluable. With today's technology, you can be a mentor and collaborator with other sales not only in your own area, but around the country.

TIP

If you're using cash boxes, make sure the boxes have a coin-tray insert.

The customer then takes the tally form to a cashier table to pay for their items. We assign two volunteers to each tally table with the specific procedure (fig. 9.2) taped to the table for reference. The tally tables need to be supplied with blank tally forms, pencils, and bags and boxes for packing customer purchases.

The selling chair is responsible for getting "seed money" for the cash boxes in many denominations of dollars and coins. Through experience, we have a set amount of bills and coins for each cash box that works for our sale. Extra coins and dollar bills are kept on hand and put in cash boxes as needed. At the end of each sale day, the cash boxes are emptied, and the starting amount is again put in each box for the next day's sale.

The cashier tables need to be placed in close proximity to the tally tables but positioned so that customers must stop at a cashier table before exiting. Cashier tables need a cash box or cash register, a calculator, pencils, pens (for customers to write checks if needed), a stack of sales receipts, and scratch paper. The cash boxes should have sufficient small bills and coins at all times. If possible, have at least one cashier table with a credit-card machine, with prominent signs indicating its location.

The cashier totals each line on the customer's book tally form, calculates the total purchase, and takes the customer's money or check. The cashier then initials a receipt for the customer to take. Tape a procedure sheet to the table to aid the cashiers (fig. 9.3). Like the tally table procedure sheet, the cashier procedure sheet is a valuable tool for the volunteers as shifts change.

Be creative with your receipts. Include information about your donation policy, upcoming sales, thanks to donors—whatever your can fit on a bookmark-size document. (See fig. 9.4 for an example from Lancaster.)

SELLING CAUTIONS AND CONCERNS

You will need a list of the volunteers who have signed up for each shift, as well as their telephone numbers. We ask our sales volunteers to check in at least fifteen minutes before their shift begins. This gives them a chance to store their personal belongings, lets the book sale leaders know that the shift is indeed covered, and gives the volunteers time to get up-to-date on what's happening at the sale. Invariably you will have someone who forgets his or her shift, or has an unavoidable family emergency. We also have several floor workers on duty who can help out if someone is late or does not show. All sellers should wear name tags. Lancaster also has aprons for the sellers to wear. These aprons have the book sale logo sewn on them, and are suitable for both men and women. Most of our sellers like to wear them.

COLLECTING AND COUNTING THE MONEY AT THE SALE

Be sure to make periodic collections from the cash boxes or registers for safety and control reasons. The selling chair or designate should perform this task. We collect the large-denomination bills and checks several times a day, as needed, during our sale. This is also a good time to see if any cash boxes are short on one-dollar bills or other change. *It is not necessary to reconcile each cash box.* Money may be exchanged between cash boxes as needed. For example, if one cash box is low on quarters, simply take quarters from another cash box. With shift changes and so many sellers, it would be a monumental task to try to reconcile each cash box every time the shifts changed. What it boils down to is this: you have to trust your sellers. Have cashiers work in teams of two for a bit of a safeguard.

If you use cash registers, as Oro Valley does, money exchanges between registers must be purchased. For example, ten one-dollar bills could be exchanged for a ten-dollar bill. This is necessary so that the cash register tape can be reconciled to the cash drawer at the end of each day. Cash pickups during the day must also be separated by register.

Using credit card machines requires running settlement tapes at the end of each day and reconciling them with the transaction slips signed by the customer. Keep an envelope in the bottom of each cash box for sellers to put the signed copy of the credit card transactions.

The collected money should be counted in a secure area at your sale site, ideally in a room that can be locked. The money can then be placed in a bank bag with a slip noting the current total.

When you are ready to make a bank deposit (at least once a day), use a deposit summary form (fig. 9.5) to

SAMPLE TALLY FORM

Price	Quantity	Total Books	Total $
$0.50	/////	5	2.50
$1.00			
$1.50			
$2.00	///// ////	9	18.00
$3.00	///	3	9.00
$4.00			
$5.00	///	3	15.00
$6.00			
$7.00			
$8.00			
$9.00			
$10.00	//	2	20.00
$11.00			
Other			
$24.00	/	1	24.00
		Total Sale	88.50
		6% Sales Tax	5.31
PD	JD	**Amount Due**	93.81
Tally Init.	Cashier Init.		

Figure 9.1 WEB
The tally person fills in book quantities only, then gives the tally form to the customer to take to the cashier for payment. The cashier then enters the totals for each line, calculates tax as applicable, takes the customer's money, and gives a receipt.

record your information. Have two people individually count and verify the information. Attach a duplicate deposit ticket, if available, or a bank receipt to your summary form. Be careful not to deposit all your small denomination bills and coins, if your sale is continuing. Periodic counting and bundling of bill denominations throughout the sale will help you make deposits quickly when needed. The interim counting also allows

SAMPLE TALLY TABLE PROCEDURE

- Customers must bring their purchases to the tally tables for items to be counted before they move on to the cashiers for payment.
- Using a Book Tally Form, record the number of books in each price line designation. One team member can call out the prices while the other records them. You may use tick marks as you process the books and then total them in the TOTAL BOOKS column. Or you may simply put the totals for each price point in the TOTAL BOOKS column. Whatever works best for your team. No overall total needed for books, just totals for each price point. Put your initials on bottom left of tally sheet. See Sample Book Tally Form at your table.
- Place the tallied purchases in bags or boxes and direct the customer to take the tally sheet to the cashier for payment.

If there's a question about a particular price, check with designated volunteer for decision/clarification. Do Not Negotiate Prices.

- Credit cards accepted
- Hours of sale are Monday 7 a.m.–9 p.m., Tuesday 9 a.m.–9 p.m., Wednesday 9 a.m.–6 p.m.

Books are full price Monday and Tuesday. Wednesday is half-price day.

ENJOY YOUR SHIFT, AND THANKS FOR VOLUNTEERING FOR THE LIBRARY!

Figure 9.2 WEB
Sample tally table procedure. Provide a procedures document at each tally table for easy reference.

CASHIER PROCEDURE

- After their purchases are tallied, customers will take purchases and tally form to Cashier Table. (If customer's purchases have not yet been tallied, direct customer to tally table.)
- On customer's Book Tally Form, calculate each line item by multiplying the total number of books on each price line by the Total Books for that line and listing the Total $ figure <u>for each line item</u>. When all lines are calculated, add up the total Sales $ and input on form. *See Sample Book Tally Form* at your table.
- Keep tally sheet in box at table.

General Information

- Checks and credit cards are accepted. Make checks payable to LPL (Lancaster Public Library). See credit card instructions below.
- DO NOT LEAVE YOUR CASH BOX/REGISTER UNATTENDED! Money will be collected regularly by staff.
- Books are full price Monday and Tuesday. Wednesday is half-price day until 1 PM. Bag sale runs from 1-6PM. $5 per our brown bag. Sale hours are Monday 7 a.m.–9 p.m., Tuesday 9 a.m.–9 p.m., Wednesday 9 a.m–6 p.m.

Credit Card Procedure

- [Specify your own credit-card procedure here.]

ENJOY YOUR SHIFT, AND THANKS FOR VOLUNTEERING FOR THE LIBRARY!

Figure 9.3 WEB
Sample cashier procedure. Provide a procedures document at each cashier table for easy reference.

you to give preliminary sales totals to your committee and volunteers. Although this is a rough count, it does give you a sense of how your sale is doing.

The deposit summary is designed to give sale-to-date information as prior deposits are added to current deposits for a cumulative total. Keep seed money repayment sepa-

rate and do not include it as part of your sale proceeds.

There are several ways that Friends groups can handle depositing book sale proceeds. Lancaster deposits book sale money directly into the library's general fund account. The library then has immediate access to the funds. We suggest you think about this for your

FRONT OF RECEIPT

BACK OF RECEIPT

FRIENDS OF THE LANCASTER PUBLIC LIBRARY 44TH ANNUAL BOOK SALE

All Proceeds
Benefit the Library

Friends of the Lancaster Public Library thank the following patrons for their contributions to the 1999 Book Sale

Arthur's Bakery
Beech Distributing Co., Inc.
The Book Nook
Boy Scout Troop #94
Clancy's Spring Water
Don's Pizza
Jacob's Family Market
Lancaster Public Work-Release
Shank's Dairy
Taylor Elementary School
Suburban Sandwich
Teamster's Local 800
Young's Freight

Thank you for YOUR help!

Paid $ _____

Seller's Initials _____

FUTURE BOOK SALES

All Proceeds
Benefit the Library

Harvest Sale
At Lancaster Public Library
125 N. Duke St., Lancaster
Friday, Nov. 12, 1999
Saturday, Nov. 13, 1999
Sunday, Nov. 14, 1999 (half-price)

45th Annual Book Sale
Monday, May 1, 2000
Tuesday, May 2, 2000
Wednesday, May 3, 2000 (half-price)

BOOKSTORE
Lancaster Public Library, 2nd Floor
Mondays, 6:00 PM–8:30 PM
Tuesdays, 10:00 AM–2:00 PM
Fridays, 10:00 AM–2:00 PM
Saturdays, 10:00 AM–2:00 PM

Book donations are accepted on the first Saturday of every month at the Book ReSort, 519 Mary Ave., Lancaster, from 10:00 AM–2:00 PM.

Figure 9.4 WEB
Sample book sale receipt.

group. Potsdam deposits their book sale proceeds into a Friends bank account and periodically gives the money to the library or buys specific items needed by the library. Oro Valley's library director is a voting member of the Friends board and helps to direct the transfer of funds as they are needed for purchasing books or other items.

Just remember that you are raising money on behalf of your library and are using books donated to the library to raise the money. The Friends are merely the conduit for getting all fund-raising money to the library. Keeping a large balance in a Friends account is contrary to your mission to support the library.

SALES TOTAL ANNOUNCEMENT

We always try to have at least a preliminary sales total to announce as the clean-up crew is finishing up the packing of leftover books. Make the announcement

BOOK SALE DEPOSIT SUMMARY

Sale Event	Spring Book Sale 1999	
Day	Monday	
Date	May 3, 1999	
Time	3:30 p.m.	
Counted By	Jane Doe	
Checked By	C. Smith	
2	$100 bills	$200.00
—	$50 bills	—
6	$20 bills	$120.00
12	$10 bills	$120.00
20	$5 bills	$100.00
—	$2 bills	—
65	$1 bills	$65.00
—	$1 coins	—
3	Halves	$1.50
80	Quarters	$20.00
200	Dimes	$20.00
60	Nickels	$3.00
85	Pennies	$0.85
	Cash Total	$650.35
	Checks Total	$310.00
	Total This Deposit	$960.35
	Cumulative Total for This Sale	$960.35

```
TAPE DEPOSIT TICKET COPY HERE
```

Figure 9.5 WEB

Sample deposit summary.

so that all the volunteers can share in the accomplishment of making money for the library.

ACCEPTING PERSONAL CHECKS

All three of our Friends groups accept personal checks for book sales. Yes, Lancaster has had a bounced check or two in our 57 years of sales, but it has not been a big problem. This is a personal decision for your group, but the increased sales and customer satisfaction, we feel, are worth the small risk.

BOOK SALE SALES TAX CALCULATION

Event: _Spring Book Sale_

Date: _May 23, 2009_

Prepared by: _J. Christie_

1. Gross sales including tax collected	$11,118.61
2. Less exempt sales	$1,080.00
3. = Sales subject to tax incl. tax collected	$10,038.61
4. Taxable sales (#3 /1.06)	$9,470.39
5. Sales tax on above (#3–#4)	$568.22
PROOF: #4 x .06	$569.22

Calculation of Gross Proceeds after Tax

1. Gross sales (from #1 above)	$11,118.61
2. Less sales tax collected (from #5 above)	$568.22
3. = Gross proceeds excluding tax	$10, 550.39

Figure 9.6 WEB

Sample tax calculation form.

BOOK SALE SALES HISTORY SUMMARY

Sale Description	Date	Location	Proceeds	Year-to-Date Total	Cumulative Total
Year End 2008	—	—	—	—	$90,568
Spring Book Sale	05/15/09	Martin's Arena	$8,810	$8,810	
Community Days Sale	07/04/09	Town Square	$1,200	$10,010	
Fall Book Sale	09/25/09	Martin's Arena	$6,580	$16,590	
Ye Olde Book Shoppe	Yr 2009	Library	$5,208	$21,798	
Internet Sales	Yr 2009	Amazon.com	$3,200	$24,998	$115,566

Figure 9.7 WEB
Sample sales history summary.

SALES TAX COLLECTION

If you're lucky, your book sale may not be subject to sales tax collection; if you're unsure, check with the taxing authorities in your state. If your state or local taxing authorities require collection of tax monies, see the sales tax calculation form (fig. 9.6). Because Lancaster has more than three annual fund-raising events, Pennsylvania law requires sales tax collection. Since Lancaster Library receives all the funds, the library controller files the book sale tax information along with the rest of the library sales tax revenue. The book sale committee must supply the library with the necessary information, including gross sales, exempt sales, and the amount of tax collected. Book dealers and store owners, who have an exemption certificate stating their purchase is for resale, are not subject to the tax. Lancaster records these exempt sales carefully so these amounts can be deducted from the gross sales to arrive at taxable sales.

 TIP

Having a mobile automated teller machine on-site can boost sales.

YEARLY SALES TOTALS

It is important and useful to keep a detailed summary of your various sales each year. This summary (fig. 9.7) should show the various sources of income in a year, plus the cumulative totals for all years. These reports are a good way of reporting book sale efforts to the Friends board, the library director, and the board of trustees. This information can also be used very effectively in your marketing for new Friends members as well as book sale promotion to the media.

It is *extremely* important to maintain the integrity of your sale. Take the necessary precautions to train your sellers about the proper way to handle customers as well as the money they are responsible for.

Make regular collections from the cash boxes so there is never a great amount sitting in the cash boxes at any time. This will ease your sellers' minds and will also give you some preliminary sales numbers to determine how your sale is progressing.

Be sure to safeguard the book sale money. Keep it locked and secure during the sale (Oro Valley Friends purchased a small vault), deposit money in the bank regularly, and have two people verify the count and deposit.

10

Encore! Encore!
Other Book Sale Opportunities

Here's your chance to be very creative! As you begin to accumulate lots of donations from your community, you may want to seek unique ways to sell some of these books. Your annual, traditional book sales are the bread-and-butter of your fund-raising, but opportunity is knocking in other areas to make even more money for your library.

MINI-SALES

There are most certainly opportunities in your community where you can sell a few boxes of books. Lancaster sells books every year at a Christmas bazaar held in a local church. The bazaar is filled with Christmas wreaths, ornaments, gifts, and "country crafts." Lancaster is the only bookseller, however, and customers flock to the book sale tables. At first we were a little embarrassed about stealing customers from the other stands until the bazaar coordinator told us she got many calls asking if this is the bazaar that sells books. The book tables were bringing book-loving customers who otherwise might not have stopped in at the bazaar. Lancaster takes selected categories

 TIP

Paperbacks sell well when the crowd is on foot, carrying their purchases.

to this sale—about twenty boxes of specific Christmas items, gift books, current best sellers, and children's and teen books. Craft books and cookbooks also sell well there. In 2010, the profit from this six-hour sale was about $1,400. We also handed out bookmarks with dates for the big spring sale, distributed information about our year-round bookstores, and signed up a new volunteer. A very productive day!

Lancaster, Potsdam, and Oro Valley often capitalize on community days. Wherever there is a crowd, we like to be there with a few tables of books appropriate for the occasion. Oro Valley has sold books at a local Saturday farmers' market near the library and at a town Christmas festival.

YEAR-ROUND BOOKSTORES

In 1995 Lancaster started a year-round used bookstore on the second floor of the library. The room was once a lovely museum area run by the Friends, but the library needed a storage area, so the room was turned into a big closet. The library director later found another solution to the storage problem and let the Friends open a used bookstore in the room. About 2,000 great books were pulled out of the warehouse, and a store was born. In keeping with the historical intent of the room, the store was named the Juliana Book Store, in honor of Juliana Penn, William Penn's granddaughter. Though no longer in its original building, the Lancaster library is 250 years old, established in the colonies in 1759. A picture of Juliana hangs in the store, and we are pretty sure she's smiling about the store's success.

The Juliana Book Store makes about $1,200 a month, and the public is delighted to be able to shop for used books on a regular basis. Not ones to rest on our laurels, in 2009 Lancaster opened a second used bookstore

 TIP

Create a "$2 Off Store Purchases" bookmark and ask the library staff to put them in books borrowed from the library. This will raise awareness of your bookstore and bring in curious customers. Create a similar coupon for the back of the customer's receipt at book sales.

in the Book ReSort warehouse where we sort books. Named the Marshall Street Book Shoppe, this new store is in a bright room with many bookshelves—about 3,000 volumes on the shelves at any one time. The store made over $16,000 in the first year of operation. The Book Shoppe is open twenty-four hours a week and staffed by two volunteers for each shift. We have one person who is paid by the Office of Aging and works twenty hours a week in the store. He's happy to have some part-time employment, and we are thankful for the twenty hours a week he gives us. See if there might be a similar opportunity in your own community. Some of this federal funding is being cut, but your state agencies or AARP may have similar programs.

Lancaster's two bookstores recently initiated a customer appreciation card for frequent shoppers. The back of the card has ten boxes where sellers stamp a library logo for every purchase of $5 or more. After accumulating ten stamps, customers get $5 off their next purchase. These frequent-shopper cards are very popular.

Potsdam Library Friends started a small bookstore in their first sorting facility and built up a regular customer base there. They have now moved to a much bigger space located in the basement of the Potsdam library, and in a recent year made about $12,000.

Oro Valley opened its first Book Shoppe in January 2006 in a small corner of the library (fig. 10.1). The Book Shoppe started in a small way with about 1,000 books for sale. Now in an expanded space, the inventory has grown to about 6,000 books, with Friends making and selling bookmarks, greeting cards, and Arizona-related canvas tote bags as well. The Book Shoppe is open forty-four hours a week. Volunteers include a manager, two assistant managers, and thirty to forty other volunteers working three-hour shifts. The Book Shoppe has been wildly successful and is Oro Valley Friends largest book-selling source, generating $54,000 in 2010.

A second bookstore, Book Shoppe Too!, opened in 2011, and serves the public about forty hours a week. This new store has a special focus on books about the Southwest and rare and collectible volumes.

These year-round bookstores provide the opportunity to put current best sellers in the stores immediately (rather than storing them away for six months until the big sale), while also allowing customers to find earlier titles by their favorite authors. The stores also provide an outlet for seasonal books and small items that tend to get lost in the big sales. And, amazingly,

Figure 10.1

The Oro Valley Book Shoppe started in a small way with about 1,000 books in a small corner of the library. Now in an expanded space, the inventory has grown to about 6,000 books.

these books regularly get donated back to the Friends to sell again and again. One of the biggest benefits is that these stores make money that flows regularly to the library and are a great training ground for supplying experienced sellers for your book sales.

SELLING BOOKS FOR DECORATIVE USE

Interior decorators, furniture stores, hotels, and even restaurants may be in the market for "pretty" books to fill empty shelves. These books do not have to be readable—they just need to look nice. When a large

hotel chain opened a new facility, Lancaster provided books to fill dozens of decorative shelves. The books provided were old law texts, unsellable old encyclopedia texts, grossly underlined books with nice covers—all items that were of no use to the book sale. The library made several hundred dollars, the hotel was pleased, and unusable items were recycled. Oro Valley has sold decorative books to real estate developers to use in their model homes. Sometimes homeowners themselves are in the market for books in bulk. An executive and his wife came to the Lancaster sale a few years ago and wanted 60 feet of books—they didn't care what—to fill bookshelves in their new house. The committee didn't try to figure this out, but just sold them the books!

BOOK DONATIONS TO OTHER NONPROFIT GROUPS

Although not a source of profit, donating books to local agencies serving your community is an excellent way to promote the library and reading. Lancaster has donated many books to nonprofit agencies that have a small library in their facility. These books are usually requested by the agencies. Lancaster also donates books to retirement homes and helps stock a library in the local prison. They always have a few boxes in their warehouse designated for these places. Oro Valley donated books to a teen correctional facility. These efforts are always much appreciated.

INTERNET SALES

There is an aura of mystery and trepidation to some about selling on the Internet. By explaining our processes, we'll show you that it's easier than you might think. There are many ways to sell books on the Internet. You could set up your own website, sell through sites such as Advanced Book Exchange, Biblio, and Alibris, as some bookstores do, or through Amazon, eBay, and other online sites. We will explain our current Internet sales methods to give you an idea of the enormous potential of the Internet marketplace, where there are *millions* of shoppers. The method you choose may be different from our methods, but the overall concept and benefits for your own library can still be achieved. We will also discuss the differences between regular sales and auction selling on the Internet.

The first step is to print out and read the registration as well as the participation agreement, which defines the terms, your rights, and the like. After reading the site agreement and reviewing the fees, set up a credit card account. This is mandatory, but you have some options of how you will pay the site fees. You will also have to designate a contact person for your online account, which should be one of your Friends volunteers. Then you select where your online fees will be charged. Many online sites charge a small fee to list items for sale.

During the registration process, you will need to select a name (member ID) where your auctions will be listed and your account profile stored. You can then begin to list items you want to offer for sale. When

 TIP

Lancaster's eBay member ID is *lancasterbooks*. Potsdam chose *potsbooks* as their member ID, and they list their books on Amazon.com. Oro Valley uses the member ID *ovbooks1* on eBay and *orovalleybooks* on Amazon. Take a look at some of these listings to get an idea of what the items look like, what kinds of books we sell on the Internet, and how we describe the books.

an item is sold, the website charges a closing fee on items sold, all noted in the agreement.

These Internet sites are easy to use. Some have a huge database of book information you can tap into without having to enter the details for many of the books you will list. We also like to include a picture of the book cover, a signature, or a unique illustration with the auction details.

On eBay about 99 percent of payments by customers for online sales are processed through PayPal. We do get occasional money orders or even individual checks for payment at the customer's request. Of course, we don't ship the books until payment has been received. This requires setting up a PayPal account—very easy—and also designating which bank account you will transfer these PayPal payments to. As your proceeds accumulate in PayPal, you must manually request that money be withdrawn from your PayPal account and transferred to your designated bank account.

Both Lancaster and Oro Valley sell through Amazon as well, and Amazon takes care of payments from the customer and sends the money directly to our accounts periodically. It is a simple and quick process to input the book information, and there is no listing fee—only a charge if the book sells. Books do not have to be relisted as they do on eBay, but rather remain on your site until you remove them. Amazon collects the funds and sends them periodically to our designated bank account, and with eBay sales we manually move the funds from PayPal to our bank account. Books to Amazon customers are shipped within two days of purchase, along with delivery confirmation.

All of Lancaster's book sale proceeds go directly to the library's general fund, per an agreement between the Friends and the library. Because of this unique arrangement, Lancaster uses a library account for Internet activities. Potsdam uses a Friends of the Library account, with all sales recorded and then money passed periodically to the library. Oro Valley's proceeds also go directly to a Friends' checking account, to be disbursed by the board after discussion with the library.

We feel that eBay and Amazon are equally easy to use. Pictures can be included, and listing is very simple. Internet sales have become an important part of our book sale structure.

Details from Our Sales

Lancaster

Lancaster started Internet sales in October 1999. We sell books on Amazon, but many of our books are now listed on eBay auctions. Amazon works for us for technical and textbooks, and also more current books. We have had great success with our more unique or older books on the auction site. We have great fun and often make more money with the auction process. Some of our books, originally listed at a price we'd be very happy with, have garnered unbelievable bids. Our volunteers really enjoy watching the listings as online bidders push the selling price up.

In Lancaster we enjoy the sheer fun and monetary benefits of watching some of our more interesting books get dozens of bids. This, of course, maximizes your selling price.

A few of Lancaster's recent interesting eBay auction items include:

Golf Architecture in America. A 1927 edition of how to lay out a golf course. We found no other copies during our Internet research before listing the book. We opened with a price of $45; the auction ended at $241.

Peregrin and the Goldfish by Mrs. Tom Seidmann-Freud. A 1929 edition of a children's book with beautiful illustrations by Sigmund Freud's niece. The complicated original German story was rewritten, at the German's request, by an American teacher, Alice Dagliesh. Dagliesh used her elementary school classes to help her write a new story by looking at the gorgeous illustrations. The book was listed on eBay for $75, got 192 hits, and sold for $1,288 to a buyer from Germany. (The buyer asked if we had another one of the same book for sale so she could buy it at the same $1,288 price. If only!)

Ghost of Lake Taraho. A very small, stapled booklet from Ralston Purina that many years ago was mailed to people who sent in Ralston cereal box tops. We don't know what wonderful book donor gave this pamphlet to us, but we thank them! Again our research found none of this title listed on the Internet. We listed the booklet for $24 and got ten bids—the winner paid us $415.00.

Obviously, we selected a few of the gems to tell you about, but many, many items we list receive multiple bids, thereby earning us a higher price.

Lancaster's online sales net profits (after the deduction of Internet fees) from 2000 to 2010 were over $107,000. We now have more researchers and listers, and our current year projection is $12,000 in sales just from the Internet.

Lancaster is also selling textbooks to Barnes & Noble online (www.barnesandnoble.com/textbookbuyback/) with great results. In the past six months at the time of this writing, we have sold nearly $1,500 of textbooks to Barnes & Noble, with many of these textbooks being not too desirable at our book sales. Barnes & Noble pays the shipping. Simply input ISBNs into their website to check whether they want the book and how much they will pay for it. Always check the prices on bookfinder.com to make sure you don't miss getting a better price at the book sale or eBay. Just remember that the B&N quote is a sure sale. We started this endeavor because of information shared by the Lewisburg (PA) Friends

 TIP

Contact and meet with other Friends groups in your area. Oro Valley started a Friends Helping Friends group with of half a dozen local libraries. They meet once a year at rotating libraries, tour the library, have a catered lunch, and discuss and share book sale information. We all can learn from each other, and our libraries will be the winners!

group, and these textbook sales have added greatly to our online profits.

Partly because of the Barnes & Noble sales but also for everyday Internet research, we are now using scanners at our computers. The library gave us a couple of old scanners they once used at the circulation desk, and they work just fine for us. Rather than having to input the 10-digit bar code manually, the scanner sends the code to your computer. These scanners save so much time on books that have bar codes. We research more items because of the ease, and we have stumbled across some astonishing finds that we probably would not have priced very high for the sale or may have even discarded.

Oro Valley

Oro Valley sells books on eBay and through Amazon. For 2010 our Internet sales were $12,088, with most of those sales coming from our Amazon listings.

One reason we prefer Amazon is that for a flat monthly fee, we can list as many books as we like. We may have over 500 books listed at any given time. Unlike our eBay items, Amazon listings remain on the site until we choose to remove them. We constantly reevaluate to be sure our pricing is competitive and remove titles as needed. These books then go to one of our bookshops or an upcoming sale. Listing on Amazon is very profitable, as we can put more books on in less time.

That said, the eBay auctions are exciting. We usually place our more collectible, complicated listings here. Recently we sold John Steinbeck's *Cup of Gold* for $1,200. One of our researchers noticed a lot of this title online, but ours had a difference: the maroon boards signified a very valuable find. She dug deeper and discovered that we did indeed have a first edition, second issue. What a find!

We also use the Barnes & Noble book buyback system, which has proven very worthwhile for us. Barcode scanners have worked well for us, too, though we prefer stand-alone rather than handheld scanners for ease of use. This selling opportunity and the scanner information came to us from Lancaster, who heard it from another Friends' book sale. Sharing our knowledge makes us all better booksellers for our libraries.

 TIP

There are many other websites that buy textbooks, including Amazon.com and webuytextbooks.com. Check out this easy and lucrative way to make a little more money from your donated books.

SELECTING APPROPRIATE BOOKS TO SELL ON THE INTERNET

We carefully select items from book donations to research for possible listing on the Internet. Often, the most successful books to offer for sale on the Internet are the old, out-of-print items that are not readily available in the marketplace. In your research you will be setting an online selling price for your book. A very useful website to help in this pricing decision is www.bookfinder.com. This website has a database of over 150 million books and pulls together many different sites that offer used books for sale. The listings give information regarding condition, first edition status, and a range of prices that booksellers are asking for editions similar to yours. These prices are well above the price you should use. On Amazon there is a feature that allows you to see the salability of your book. Remember that these other sellers had to buy their books (yours are free), and they often have expenses such as payroll and rent. You have very little overhead expense, so you can keep your prices a little lower than these bookstores and dealers. Be conscious of the fact that all the books you are seeing on these websites are not sold! Your own experience will also help you price your books so they will sell. See appendix D, "Internet Resources," for a listing of helpful websites.

We designed an Internet input form (fig. 10.2) for our volunteer researchers to list elements of the books selected to be sold online. Serious book collectors are on the Internet, and you will need to learn to describe your books carefully using some of the book terms listed in the glossary in appendix B. Every defect must be noted, and you will learn how to grade your books using the glossary found on the www.bookfinder.com website. Print out the portion showing book sizes and condition of books from that website's glossary, and keep these sections handy as you process your books. You can train volunteer researchers to help look up the book information, fill out the input form, and put the input form in the front of the book for your volunteer "experts" to review before the book is listed for sale online.

LISTING BOOKS ONLINE

Armed with books and completed input forms, you are now ready to list your items. Follow the steps for listing an item on your chosen website, describe your book completely and fairly, and sit back and wait for it to sell. Be sure to note in your listing that all proceeds benefit your library. This library notation brings shoppers to us and has even generated monetary donations to our library. People have this great affection and support for libraries in general, and you will want to include this important fact in your listing.

SHIPPING INTERNET BOOKS

Books we sell on the Internet are shipped through the U.S. Postal Service, mostly through media mail and sometimes Priority Mail. Priority Mail boxes and packaging supplies are free from the post office. Check online for postal rates at www.usps.com or get a rate schedule from your local post office. Most online selling sites have limits on prices you can charge for shipping your item domestically. You can charge more for international shipping once you know the buyer's mailing address. But for domestic shipments that you think might be higher than the website's shipping limit, you will need to add a few dollars to your asking price for the book to cover the additional shipping costs you know you will incur.

Don't hesitate to sell your books worldwide, as the shipping and customs declarations are easy to complete. We have sold books around the world, to Japan, Tahiti, France, Australia, Italy, Kenya, Brazil—in fact, to every continent except Antarctica! The global economy works to your advantage, as many of these books are just not available in foreign countries.

INTERNET INPUT FORM

Title _____

Author _____

Illustrator _____

Publisher/year _____

Edition/printing _____

ISBN _____

Book condition _____

_____

_____

_____

Brief story description _____

_____

_____

_____

Estimated book sale price _____

Suggested online price _____

Prices and quantity found online for similar items:

Bookfinder.com _____

Addall.com _____

Other _____

Prepared by _____

Reviewed by _____

Figure 10.2 🌐

Sample Internet input form. (Reduce/increase write-on lines/ spacing as needed to fit vertical format).

We wrap the books in bubble-wrap to protect them, and we use labels, boxes, and envelopes supplied by the U.S. Postal Service for priority mail. These shipping materials can be obtained at your local post office or can be ordered online from the Postal Service at www .supplies.usps.com. The materials are delivered free of charge right to your door. Book-rate padded envelopes

BOOKS SOLD ON EBAY AUCTIONS—LANCBOOKS

Title/Author	Book Sale Estimate	Min. Bid	No. of Bids	Winning Bid	Fees Billed		Net Profit	Amt. Over Book Sale Estimate	Pmt. Rec'd	Sale Date	Shipping Location	Shipping Cost
					Ave. Post	Auction						
Rabbit Is Rich (Updike signed)	24.00	40.00	5	55.00	1.00	2.75	51.25	27.25	59.00	01/31/08	MN	4.00
Flash Gordon: Caverns of Mongo	8.00	22.00	7	46.99	1.00	2.35	43.64	35.64	49.99	02/05/08	CA	4.00
Royalty Rates for Licensing	4.00	24.00	4	51.00	1.00	2.55	47.45	43.45	55.00	02/10/08	WA	4.00
Modern Herbal (2 vol.)	15.00	30.00	1	30.00	1.00	1.50	27.50	12.50	34.00	02/25/08	Canada	12.00
Gettysburg: Day Two	40.00	90.00	6	150.00	1.00	7.50	141.50	101.50	154.00	03/26/08	PA	6.00
Freddy and the Popinjay	6.00	20.00	1	20.00	1.00	1.00	18.00	12.00	24.00	03/26/08	WV	3.00
Life Story of Ringling Bros.	16.00	40.00	1	40.00	1.00	2.00	37.00	21.00	44.00	04/07/08	FL	4.00
Classic Soda Machines	5.00	15.00	1	15.00	1.00	0.75	13.25	8.25	19.00	04/07/08	GA	8.50
Maori Mothers	4.00	18.00	2	30.00	1.00	1.50	27.50	23.50	42.00	05/10/08	Australia	12.00
TOTAL	122.00	299.00		437.99			407.09	285.09	480.99			57.50

Figure 10.3 WEB
Sample Internet sales log.

TIP

Ask local stores such as Marshall's or Kmart or craft shops such as Michael's to save bubble wrap for you to recycle as packing material for online sales.

can be purchased at office supply stores or online. At Lancaster we use a lot of bubble wrap, but we have never had to buy any, as we have a volunteer who has lined up a few stores that save it for her to pick up. These stores simply throw the bubble wrap in a large plastic bag, and she sorts through it and rolls it up by size for use by packers.

WHEN YOUR BOOK SELLS

If your auction closes without a bid, you can relist the item easily on eBay. Amazon items remain listed until you close them. You may want to consider dropping the price, revising your description, or removing the item from your listing if it isn't selling. New shoppers come online every day, and patience often pays off.

When your book sells, you and the buyer are both notified by e-mail. As the seller, we send a congratulatory e-mail to the winner. We also input positive feedback for the buyer on Internet items. Lancaster keeps a summary report of Internet sales (fig. 10.3), which lists the expected book sale price, how many bids the item received, and the final selling price. They also deduct an average auction price and website fees to show a net profit on each book sold. The form also has a place to record when the book is paid and when shipped.

INTERNET POTENTIAL

Reaching the enormous audience of the Internet expands your marketing base by millions of people. Only your time resources will limit your sales. Out-of-print books in particular are in high demand online, and your library can greatly benefit from your Internet efforts.

A Note from the Authors

The proven tools and strategies to start a new book sale or expand an existing sale are here for you to use and adapt to your unique situation. Getting or growing your supply of book donations, volunteers, and dollars raised will benefit your library and community.

While a lot of work is involved in sorting, pricing, and ultimately selling books, we have had a lot of fun along the way—forging new relationships, developing new skills, and feeling great about our volunteer team making our community a better place to live.

We wish you much success and fulfillment as you embark on your great book-selling adventure!

Appendix A

Resource Information

BOOK SALE SUPPLIES—POSSIBLE SOURCES

Listed below are some suppliers we use for our book sale, along with the supplies we typically get from each. Your needs will vary depending on the size of your sale and how you choose to operate. This list is only a general guide. We are not associated with any of the vendors. They are simply places we have discovered that have good prices and quality for our needs. Whenever possible, we solicit donations or buy supplies at local discount stores. Sometimes your library can get good discounts for you, so check prices with them before seeking supplies elsewhere.

Reliable Office Supplies
Ottawa, IL
800-735-4000
www.reliable.com

Reliable's name really is indicative of their service level. The supplies come to your door with no shipping charges and usually arrive within two to three days

Sealing tape and **handheld tape dispensers.** We sort all year long and seal the completed boxes going to our storage room, since the boxes will be stored for several months. After several trials, we settled on Reliable's premium grade rolls of tan sealing tape. We did try a local cheaper brand, but it was unsatisfactory.

Color-coded removable dots. We use white or yellow dots to price books with glossy covers, boxed book sets, records, compact discs, and the like.

Fine Sharpie markers. We do buy the markers locally when we find a good price.

Brodart Library Supplies
Williamsport, PA
888–820–4377
www.shopbrodart.com

Book jacket covers. Archival-quality plastic jackets are used to cover the dust jackets of some of our higher-priced books, especially for some of the books we sell on the Internet. These jackets serve two purposes: they protect pristine dust jackets so they stay that way, but they also can hold together a desirable dust jacket that is fragile and you want to protect from further damage.

Book-repair tape. This acid-free tape does a nice job on simple repairs. Brodart sent us a free pamphlet on book repairs long ago. It doesn't seem to be available on their website anymore, although they are selling an expensive DVD on the topic. Find someone locally who can show you a few basics about simple repairs. Your library may have a staff person who is knowledgeable about them.

Bags Unlimited
Rochester, NY
800–767–BAGS
www.bagsunlimited.com

Polyethylene sleeves. These come in a myriad of sizes and are great for sheet music, collectible comic books, valuable old cooking pamphlets, and other similar items. They cost a few cents apiece but can add several dollars to your asking price. Also, fragile items have a fighting chance to stay intact at the sale if you put them in a poly bag and put a sticker price on the front. The shopper can see the item and price at a glance and will open the bag for further inspection only if interested. Try to put the price on the item itself as well, as we have seen a few discarded bags at the sale in the past with no item inside. With the price on the outside of the bag too, shoppers don't need to disturb the item if they are not interested after seeing the price.

Album sleeves. Lancaster receives many donated records. Our record sorters decided to enhance the presentation of some of the higher-priced records. Polyethylene album sleeves cover the very best or collectible album covers; we do not use many gold sleeves for 45 records but have sold some very collectible rock 'n' roll 45s for a nice price.

Appendix B

Common Book Collecting and Book Condition Terms

Americana
    books on America, its history, and its people

-ana
    suffix referring to any kind of material about the author or subject to which it is attached. For example, *Steinbeckana* means any book or item about Steinbeck, but not by him.

association copy
    book once owned by someone associated with the author or by the author himself

book club
    edition printed for a book club. Usually of cheaper materials, although some book club editions are the first editions of an author's work.

bookplate
    paper label posted inside the front cover to denote ownership. Some bookplates are highly collectible, particularly those signed by the artist.
    The most prized bookplate in the United States is that of George Washington.

chipped
    dust jacket with small pieces missing or frayed

colophon
    reference from a printer or publisher at the end of a book, often on desirable limited editions

deckle edges
    uncut or untrimmed edges. Desirable.

dust jacket

(also *dust wrapper*) the decorative paper wrapper placed around a book to protect the binding. First used in nineteenth century. Considered an integral part of a book by collectors. Premium prices can be asked for early books in original jackets. If the dust jacket is fragile, or if it is highly collectible, a clear plastic dust jacket protector should be placed over the paper jacket. (See appendix A on where to purchase protectors.)

end papers

blank leaves at the beginning and ending of a book, with one-half pasted to the inside cover and the other half free. Blank leaves other than these end papers are called *flyleaves*.

ephemera

pamphlets, handbills, and broadsides (unfolded sheet of paper with printed matter on one side). Greek for "something that disappears quickly." Some ephemera are highly collectible. These items should be placed in plastic bags for protection during your sale.

errata

mistakes or errors in printing. Sometimes errata slips are laid in loosely or glued (tipped) in book by the publisher, when errors are discovered too late to correct but prior to publication. These slips are easily lost and therefore are a plus when they are included.

ex-library

book that is identified as having been in a library or other lending institution. Usually well worn and marked, and may have code pockets, call letters, etc. Occasionally, however, these books are signed or first editions, and therefore collectible.

first edition

first appearance of a work in book form

first trade edition

first edition of a work that previously appeared initially in a limited edition or privately printed format

folio

relatively large book, approximately 12-by-15 inches

foxing

brown spotting and blotches on the paper caused by chemical reaction. Often found in nineteenth century books.

frontispiece

illustration at beginning of book, usually facing the title page

half leather

(also *half binding*). Binding where the leather covers the spine of the book and triangular pieces of leather are on the outer corners. The rest of the binding is cloth or paper.

hinge

joint of the book binding that bends when the book is opened. Gets lots of wear and tear; thus there are many defective hinges.

incunabula

books from the earliest period of print (fifteenth century)

inscribed copy

books with an inscription (comment or phrase) written by the author

limited edition

edition of a book limited to a given number of copies and often signed by the author or illustrator. These limited editions are usually printed on better paper than trade editions and have more expensive bindings. Occasionally limited editions are issued in a slipcase (*publisher's box*).

marbled

paper printed with imitation marble pattern. Very popular for end papers in the nineteenth century. Today they are used in some deluxe editions.

mint copy

book in perfect condition, as fresh as the day it was issued

morocco

type of leather made from goatskins—durable and beautiful. Can be dyed in a variety of colors, red, brown, green, and black being the most common.

out-of-print

book no longer available from the publisher. Many of your sale books will be in this category.

pirated edition

edition produced without consent of the author or owner of the copyright. Illegal and unauthorized. Many pirated editions are printed in Taiwan and are, curiously, collectible.

points

features such as corrections, misprints, and advertisements that distinguish one issue or edition of the book from another. Points are well known by collectors, and as such, should be included in your publicity.

presentation copy

copy of a book clearly presented by the author to an acquaintance, usually with an inscription. A mere signature is not a presentation copy.

private press

small press, usually devoted to production of small quantities of finely printed books. Many people collect these high-quality *press books*. Many communities have local, sometimes *out-of-business* small presses that would also be highly collectible in your own area.

provenance

history of a book's ownership. Determined by book plates or the owners' names written in the book

remainder

when a book is no longer selling, the publisher may get rid of overstock by *remaindering* the title. These remaindered books are sold in quantity at a reduced price. Usually have a felt marker slash on the bottom of the closed pages. Not highly desirable.

review copy

copy sent to a critic or reviewer before publication. Sometimes the review copy is the earliest issue. Very collectible if by a known author. Review (often called *advance*) copies can be priced a little higher.

rubbed

scuffed binding

salesman dummy

mock-up of a book used by salesmen in the late 1800s or early 1900s to show buyers what the book would look like. Sometimes has sample bindings, then sample pages followed by blank pages.

shaken book that is loose between its covers

slipcase

box into which a book can be slipped for protection

sunned

faded from exposure to light or direct sunlight. Usually occurs on the spine, even through dust jackets.

Appendix C

Collectible Books

This list is our current sorting-room reference for collectible books. It is by no means all-inclusive. We constantly add new items to the list and also delete items as appropriate. An editable version is available for download at alaeditions.org/webextras. You will want to add regional books and your own local authors to the list. Update your version regularly as you learn more about collectibles.

Any prices listed here are only guidelines. Your region and the specific customers at your sale in any given year will determine the price at which your books will sell.

A

Advance reading copies—any author, but more famous authors worth more
Alger, Horatio
Alice in Wonderland books
All-About series
Almanacs—1800s or early 1900s
American Girl
American Guide Series
Cherry Ames series
Amish-related
Joan Walsh Anglund—little gift books
Annals of the Conestoga Valley—$400 to $600—PA local
Annotated books—ALL
Antiques—also Furniture refinishing

Apocrypha—biblical writings of doubtful authority, but collectible

Appleton's Travel Guides

Architecture books

Atwood, Margaret—some first editions

Audel's Carpenter's and Builder's Guides

Auto and Auto Racing books—books about vintage cars very desirable

Autographed books—value depends on celebrity

Avedon, Richard—photographer

B

Baedeker's Travel Books—Before 1920

Ballantine paperbacks—WWII—$3 to $10, depending on subject

Bangs, John Kendrick—any

Baseball—nicer books

Beckett, Samuel—any

Bemelmans, Ludwig—any

Bicycling—early books

Black's Law Dictionary

Bobbsey Twins series

Bodkin, B. A.—*American Folklore*

Book collecting, publishing, etc.

Boy Scout manuals—old (The Golden Jubilee edition worth $150!)

Brautigan, Richard—any, even paperbacks

Breen, Walter—*U. S. Coins*

British Isles Travel & History by F. Fraser Darling

"Buddy" series

Burgess, Thornton

C

Caldecott-Award winners

Car racing—the older the better

Catch-22 by Joseph Heller first edition

Caton, Bruce—all

Chandler, Raymond—first editions

Chandler, Roy—*Perry Public History*

Cheever, John—first editions

Chilton auto repair books

Circus books—including programs

Civil War books

Clancy, Tom—first editions (NOTE: *Hunt for Red October* first edition worth a lot!)

Coffee-table books—oversize, often beautiful books—many can get premium price

Community Historian's Annual

Concordances—Religion

Cookbooks—also advertising pamphlets from 1940 and earlier

Currier & Ives

D

Dahl, Roald—all

De Angeli, Marguerite—all

Decoys—any books

Dell—10-cent paperbacks and first printing 25-cent

Dick and Jane readers—good condition command about $30

Nancy Drew series—even new ones

Dr. Seuss—hardbacks

Dunbar, Paul—black author—any

Dungeons and Dragons—All

Durant, Will—*Story of Civilization*

E

Egyptology

Evergreen Review

F

Fairs and Exhibition books—e.g., St. Louis World's Fair

Farm Engines

First Editions—famous, popular authors

Fisher, M. F. K.—Cooking criticism

Fishermen's Encyclopedia and other fishing

Folio Society books

Folk Art

Ford, Henry—*International Jew*—4-volume paperback

Foxfire Books—$3 to $4

Frances, Mary—Sewing or Cooking

Franklin Library editions

Freeman, Douglas—*Lee's Lieutenant*

Freeman, Douglas—*Robert E. Lee*

Freeman, Douglas—*Washington* (7 Volumes)

Freud, Sigmund—all books

Furniture refinishing

G

Gehman, Richard—local PA author—pricey
Genealogy books
Gibran, Kahil—$2 and up
Girl Scout handbooks—1950 and older
Golden Books—first printings. See resource listing
    for reference
Gone with the Wind—first edition hardback—May 1936
Gone with the Wind—all other hardbacks—about $8.
    Also movie edition
Gorey, Edward—authored or illustrated by him
Graphic Novels
Grey, Zane—any hardbacks
Grove Press books
Gun books

H

Happy Hollisters
Hardy Boys series—even new ones
Harris, Joel Chandler
Haynes auto repair books
Hearn, Lafcadio—Japan or other ($25+)
Heller, Joseph—*Catch-22*—also his other first editions
Herb books
Hillyer, V. M.—*Child's History*
Hoffman, Abbie—any
Horse books
Hubbard, Elbert—Roycroft Press books

I

Illustrators:
    Howard Chandler Christy
    Harrison Fisher
    Edward Gorey
    Rockwell Kent
    Lois Lenski
    Peter Max
    Maxfield Parrish
    Frederick Remington
    Arthur Rackham
    Charles Robinson
    Norman Rockwell
    Eric Sloane
    N. C. and Andrew Wyeth

Indians (North American)—most books
Int'l Correspondence School—old ones

J

Janson's *History of Art*
Jeffers, Robinson—poet
Johnson, Osa—any

K

Kelly, Walt (POGO books)
Kent, Rockwell
Kentucky Rifles
Kerouac, Jack—any, including paperbacks
Kipling, Rudyard

L

Lakeside Press—any
L'Amour, Louis—any hardbacks
Lancaster Public Historical Society Journals—PA local
Landmark series—juvenile
Lawrence, T. E.—any
Chiang Lee
Lemony Snicket
Little Leather series
Local interest—authors or subjects: You will want to
    add your own regional list, although most regional
    items are desirable
    Pennsylvania
        Amish
        Charles DeMuth
        Wallace Fisher
        Richard Gehman
        Mennonites
        Earl Rebman
        Slaymaker
    New York
        Adirondack
        American Indian lore
        Frederick Remington
        St. Lawrence River
        Ray Whalen
    Arizona
        Baxter Black
        Jan Cleere

Tony Hillerman
J. A. Jantz
Mata Ortiz Pottery
Guy Porfirio
Louis Alberto Urea
Loeb Classical Library—$3 to $8
Lossing, Benson—historical U.S. books
Lovecraft, H.P.—sci-fi

M

Machinist's Handbooks
Magic—any books
Man, Myth & Magic—20-volume set
Mann, Thomas—any hardbacks
Maps—antique or railroad types
McPhee, John—most hardbacks
McSweeney's—any
Mencken, H. L.—any
Mennonites—any, especially Weaverland
Merton, Thomas—photography
Metals—any books
Metropolitan Museum books
Millay, Edna St. Vincent—poet
Modern Library—old ones with dust jacket
Movie editions of novels
Myers, Anna B.—*I Lift My Lamp*
Mystery—in dust jackets or first editions from 1940
   and earlier
   Agatha Christie
   Raymond Chandler
   Ellery Queen
   Mickey Spillane
   Rex Stout

N

Nature and wildlife—any regional
Newbery-Award winners

O

Oates, Joyce Carol—first editions
Occult—any

O'Keeffe, Georgia
Olympic games memorabilia
On The Road—Jack Kerouac (Beat Generation), even
   paperback

P

Peter Pauper Press—any
Photographers
   Ansel Adams
   Richard Avedon
   David Douglas Duncan
   Thomas Merton
   Edward Steichen
Photoplay editions
Piper, Watty—any children's
POGO books, Walt Kelly
Pop-up books—any, old or new
Potter, Harry
Power of Myth—Joseph Campbell
Printing—books about
Pynchon, Thomas—any hardbacks
Pyramid Power

Q

Queen, Ellery—first edition hardbacks

R

Railways Guide—timetables, etc.
Readers, elementary—20th century in color
Rice, Ann—first edition hardbacks
Rifles, guns—any books
Rivers of America series
Rodale Press—early books
The Rosetti's
Rubin, Jerry—60s stuff

S

Salesmen's dummy copies—have sample bindings
Saturday Night Live
Scoutmaster handbooks

Service, Robert
Dr. Seuss—older hardbacks
Shipbuilding—any
Signed copies by author
Silverstein, Shel
Sixties (1960s)—Beat Generation stuff—Ginsberg,
  Kerouac, Abbie Hoffman, etc.
Slipcase books—(in cardboard casings)
Sloane, Eric—author, illustrator
Starrett, Vincent—cult books
Steal This Book—Abbie Hoffman
Steichen, Edward—photographer
Stevenson, D. E.
Stewart, Martha
Stuart, Jessie—all
Submarines
Summers, Montague—*Vampires*
Sunbonnet books
Tom Swift
Swords—any books

T

Taber, Gladys—any books
Tarzan—including paperbacks
Temple, Shirley—any books
Thomas the Train
Thompson, Hunter—*Curse of Lono* paperback
Treason Trials—local interest
Tuchman, Barbara—hardbacks
Tyler, Anne—first editions

U

Ulysses—James Joyce
Uncle Remus
Uncle Wiggily
University Press books
Updike, John—hardback novels

V

Vampire books
Van Loon—any
Vietnam books
Vogue Fashion books

W

War books—any
Watchtower hardbacks—pre-1960
Weathervanes—any books
Weaverland Mennonites—any
West VA Pulp & Paper Christmas annuals
Wodehouse, P. G.—first edition hardbacks
WPA guides

Z

Zane Grey—any
Zen and the Art of Motorcycle Maintenance—Robert Pirsig
Zen Buddhism—any

Appendix D

Internet Resources

The Internet can be a valuable tool for your book sale activities. Information on special books and their value is right at your fingertips. In years past we had to purchase (if we could even find them) the resource books and data needed to help us set prices on those special books in our sale.

A FEW HELPFUL SITES

Listed here are a few of our favorite websites. A computer-literate volunteer in your own organization will find dozens more sites that will be beneficial to you.

www.bookfinder.com

Book search engine. This website searches about 10,000 bookstores and online selling sites from across the world. The worldwide marketplace is at your fingertips. There are over 150 million books in its database. This website will put you in touch with what used bookstores and online sellers are offering and at what price. A book's condition plays an important role in pricing, and you will be able to see the points and other features that make books more valuable and can command premium prices. Professionals in the used book business frequent this site.

A few caveats as you use this site as a guideline to price some of your special books. When searching for your title and author, also indicate on the search page that your book is used and whether it is hardback or paperback. When the listing comes up, carefully read the details of offered books and find about where your book falls in the list. Do you have a dust jacket? Is yours a first edition? (See our pricing guide resource listing for a guide to identifying first editions.) What is your book's overall condition? Check out our book terms glossary in appendix B for help in understanding terms you will see in some book listings. Bookfinder's website also has a more extensive glossary on their home page. Get familiar with these description terms.

Once you have determined the Internet asking price for a book similar to yours, we suggest pricing your book at about a third of the Internet asking price. Before finalizing the price, you can adjust it upward or downward depending on the quantity of this title available online. If the book is fairly scarce with less than ten offerings, you can add a few dollars to your asking price. Be sure to look over the search list for duplicate listings, as this site picks up listings from many different sites, and some booksellers list on multiple sites. This site does not pick up eBay listings.

www.booksalefinder.com

Listing of book sales and bookstores run by nonprofit organizations. The site offers free listings to nonprofits; sales are listed by state and by date. Detailed information includes sales hours, prices, and volume of books. One of your volunteers would probably enjoy gathering this information for your organization. Include an Internet contact address for your sale. The Internet gets your sale information out to the whole country! Lancaster gets shoppers from all over the United States who have discovered our sale through booksalefinder.com. (On the first day of our sale one year, a volunteer walked around the parking lot and found license plates from twenty-eight states!) Updates are frequent on this site. You can also use these sales listings to visit book sales near you, or have committee members check out sales while they're traveling or on vacation. Good source of new ideas.

www.addall.com and www.bn.com (used books sections)

These websites, similar to www.bookfinder.com, list used books for sale. Good for reference and research. We've found that these two websites tend to have slightly higher prices than bookfinder.com, and you should not expect to sell at these inflated prices. Occasionally an obscure item will be on these sites and not on the bookfinder site.

www.translate.google.com and www.babelfish.yahoo.com

Two useful websites for translating to and from different languages. Got a book in German and don't know what it's about? These sites can help.

www.guernsey.net/~sgibbs/roman.html

Roman numeral and date conversion website. Very useful when you can't figure out publication dates that are listed in a book as Roman numerals.

www.supplies.usps.com

Site where we order our Internet priority mail packaging and shipping supplies. These supplies are free and are delivered to your door.

www.purplehousepress.com/sig.html, www.fadedgiant.net, and www.emptymirrorbooks.com

Sites with examples of author signatures to help verify if your signature is genuine. Be aware that unless you actually see the person sign the book, there is little proof that you have an authentic signature. You may get books donated that have an *Autographed Copy* decal on the front, which will give you some assurance of authenticity. When the author's signature looks authentic from our research, we sell it as signed. An inscription by the author in the book also adds more value.

redrosebooks@aol.com

Our e-mail address. Send us your questions and comments about *A Book Sale How-To Guide.*

Appendix E

Pricing Guide Resources

There are many pricing guides to assist you in charging fair but sellable prices for your rare and collectible books. Listed below are several books we use regularly. You should seek out others that will cover specific topics that interest you and that you feel comfortable using. Prices listed in these resource books are not what you can charge at your sale; they are merely guidelines and reference points. We have become knowledgeable about pricing books through research and many years of experience selling books. Besides the resource books listed below, refer to our listing of Internet sites to guide you in the critical task of pricing your books.

Ahearn, Allen and Patricia. *Collected Books: The Guide to Values, 1998 Edition.* **New York: G. P. Putnam's Sons, 1995.**

Helps identify authors' first books (very desirable to collectors) and is also helpful to use as a guide for pricing. The prices listed are *not* normal book sale prices, and you cannot expect to match them. Except for very unusual items that will always command a good price, a rough guideline would be about a third of the price listed.

McBride, Bill (compiler). *A Pocket Guide to the Identification of First Editions.* **Louisville, KY: General Printing, 1995.**

Extremely useful for correctly identifying first editions of hardback and paperback books. The author clearly states that this is a very confusing area with many exceptions. This reference tells you if your book is most likely a first edition. Many book collectors use this guide as a reference tool, and you should become familiar with it.

Greason, Rebecca. *Tomart's Price Guide to Golden Book Collectibles.* **Radnor, PA: Wallace-Homestead Book Company, 1991.**

Santi, Steve. *Collecting Little Golden Books.* **Florence, AL: Books Americana, 1994.**

These two books are great resources for pricing Golden Books, which are becoming increasingly collectible. Don't miss the opportunity to get a fair price for these children's books. You can bet that many customers at your sale will know what they're worth.

Allen, Colonel Bob. *A Guide to Collecting Cookbooks.* **Paducah, KY: Schroeder Publishing, 1998**

This book is a good resource for pricing cookbooks and cooking pamphlets. Do you have a 1909 copy of Jell-O Desserts of the World pamphlet? The suggested guideline value is $75. We would probably try to sell it for $25, after placing it in a polyethylene bag for protection. Old cooking pamphlets in good condition are highly collectible. We have carefully trained our sorters not to throw these away, but instead to put them in a special place for later research.

You will have fun researching your own special areas of interest. Check your local library, bookstores, or online for books about *your* interests.

Index

About the Authors

Pat Ditzler is the current chair of the Lancaster, PA, book sale. She has worked with the Lancaster sale for twenty-six years in many capacities, including chairing the sale six times. Ditzler is a retired accounting analyst for Armstrong World Industries and is past president of the Lancaster Public Library board of trustees, serving as a trustee for five years. The State of Pennsylvania Citizens for Better Libraries presented a Lifetime Achievement Award to Ditzler for 2010 Volunteer of the Year. Her current aim is for hundreds of book sales to begin or expand across America in support of libraries.

JoAnn Dumas is a retired branch manager with Key Bank of New York State. She is Ditzler's sister, and she helped with the Lancaster book sale for many years. Dumas inspired the Friends of the Potsdam Public Library to adopt ideas from the Lancaster sale to begin their ongoing book sales. Since then the Friends group has grown and the community has rallied around this successful project. In 2002, Dumas retired and moved to Arizona, where she helped to reorganize the new Friends of the Oro Valley Public Library book sales. She has been recognized by the library and the Town of Oro Valley for her efforts in their success. She continues to volunteer with and mentor the book sales, serving on the Friends board as director of book sale operations. In 2011 Dumas was honored as Volunteer of the Decade by the Oro Valley Friends.

The authors have been guest speakers at national, state, and local library conferences.

40 00